CAMBRIDGE NATIONAL LEVEL 1 / LEVEL 2

Engineering Design

Student Book

Stuart Peet

Contents

Acknowledgements

The authors and publishers acknowledge the following sources of copyright material and are grateful for the permissions granted. While every effort has been made, it has not always been possible to identify the sources of all the material used, or to trace all copyright holders. If any omissions are brought to our notice, we will be happy to include the appropriate acknowledgements on reprinting.

Thanks to the following for permission to reproduce images:

Cover Talaj/GI; *Inside* **R038 TA1:** Adventtr/GI; Monty Rakusen/GI; Maximimages.com/Alamy Stock Photo; Ondacaracola Photography/GI; ANP/GI; RgStudio/GI; Iuliia Bondar/GI; Dean Mouhtaropoulos/GI; Gorodenkoff/GI; Ijubaphoto/GI; Sally Anscombe/GI; MoMo Productions/GI; Siede Preis/GI; David Malan/GI; Daniel Grizelj/GI; T3 Magazine/GI; Gandee Vasan/GI; Mevans/GI; Andriy Onufriyenko/GI; Simonkr/GI; Bloomberg/GI; Georgijevic/GI; **TA2:** Luis Alvarez/GI; Wiredtoseephotography/GI; Nika Boyce Studios/GI; Luca Sage/GI; Xia yuan/GI; DekiArt/GI; Ladislav Kubeš/GI; Prasit photo/GI; Annie Otzen/GI; Monty Rakusen/GI (x2); Thomas Heitz/GI; Enrique Alcala/EyeEm/GI; Oscar Wong/GI; BSI Kitemark logo is used with permission from the British Standards Institution; CE Symbol © European Union; UKCA mark © Crown copyright; The ISO logo is reproduced with the permission of the International Organization for Standardization, ISO. Copyright remains with ISO; The Lion Mark is used by permission of the British Toy and Hobby Association (BTHA); Nitat Termmee/GI; Radharc Images/Alamy Stock Photo; OsakaWayne Studios/GI; Dougal Waters/GI; Skhoward/GI; IndiaPix/IndiaPicture/GI; Filadendron/GI; Jupiterimages/GI; Sinology/GI; Anna Efetova/GI; Justin Paget/GI; **TA3:** Prapass Pulsub/GI; Mathisworks/GI; OktalStudio/GI; Fig 1.65 Image of Assembly drawing used with the permission of The Ohio State University College of Engineering; michael1959/GI; Steve Gorton/GI; ClarkandCompany/GI; Laurence Dutton/GI; **TA4:** Sunwoo Jung/GI; Kittiphat Abhiratvorakul/GI; Neustockimages/GI; Poba/GI; Huntstock/GI; Maciej Frolow/GI; Pablo_rodriguez1/GI; Richard Drury/GI; Luis Alvarez/GI; SDI Productions/GI; **R039 TA1:** Lane Oatey/GI; Carol Yepes/GI; Priscila Zambotto/GI; Mecaleha/GI; KeithBishop/GI; sayhmog/GI; SireAnko/GI; cako74/GI; Mark Garlick/GI; Nicolas_/GI; **TA2:** Alys Tomlinson/GI; Andrew Holt/GI; John Slater/GI; **TA3:** Monty Rakusen/GI; Image Source/GI; vm/GI; **R040 TA1:** Bloom Productions/GI; Maskot/GI; 10'000 Hours/GI; Craig Hastings/GI; Jordan Lye/GI; Buena Vista Images/GI; MirageC/GI; Gary Yeowell/GI; Christina Reichl Photography/GI; Extreme-Photographer/GI; Delihayat/GI; Daniel Grizelj/GI; Renaud Philippe/GI; Jose Bispo/GI; **TA2:** Pinstock/GI; SolStock/GI; OsakaWayne Studios/GI; S-cphoto/GI; Enviromantic/GI; Monty Rakusen/GI; Andrewhoughton/GI; Taiyou Nomachi/GI; Vladimir Zakharov/GI; Scott Barbour/GI

Key GI = Getty Images

About your Cambridge National Engineering Design course and qualification

Today's society benefits from many incredible products, from the latest smartphone to NASA Rovers and renewable technologies. All of these products have been carefully designed by engineers using the same knowledge and skills you will learn as you take this course. You may want to specialise in one of the many sectors that use the skills of engineering, such as working for a technology company or advertising, but you will benefit from having experience of the same design skills and knowledge that these engineers use.

During your Engineering Design course, you will learn about the tools and techniques that are needed to follow a career in engineering and product design. You'll have a chance to develop skills relevant for a range of roles while developing product design strategies, planning and creating detailed engineering drawings and planning, creating and reviewing original products.

How you will be assessed

You have to complete three mandatory units.

- R038: Principles of engineering design. You will take a written exam for this unit. The exam lasts for 1 hour 15 minutes, and is worth 70 marks. The exam is set and marked by OCR.

- R039: Communicating designs. You will be given an assignment to complete for this unit, which is worth 60 marks.

- R040: Design, evaluation and modelling. You will be given an assignment to complete for this unit, which is worth 60 marks.

How to use this book

Throughout this book, you will notice lots of different features that will help your learning. These are explained below.

These features at the start of each unit give you guidance on the topic area, what you will learn and how you will be assessed.

Thought-provoking questions at the start of units and topics will get you thinking about the subject.

Principles of engineering design **TA1**

What will you learn in this unit?

Whether you are aiming to become a designer or an engineer, you need to know about how products are designed and the different factors that influence their design, as well as how they are communicated, tested and evaluated. This will provide understanding that underpins the skills you will use in the other units of this course. In this unit, you will learn about the design process and all the stages that are involved.

In this unit you will learn about:

- different design strategies and when they are used **TA1**
- the stages of the iterative design process **TA1**
- types of criteria included in a design specification **TA2**
- how manufacturing and other considerations influence design **TA2**
- types of drawing used to communicate designs **TA3**
- methods of modelling and evaluating design ideas **TA4**.

How you will be assessed

This unit will be externally assessed by a one-hour 15-minute written exam that is worth 40% of your overall mark for this qualification. The exam includes two parts: a first section with ten multiple choice questions and a second section with short answer and extended response questions. In the exam, you will be expected to show that you understand this unit by answering questions about the design process and all of the stages that this involves.

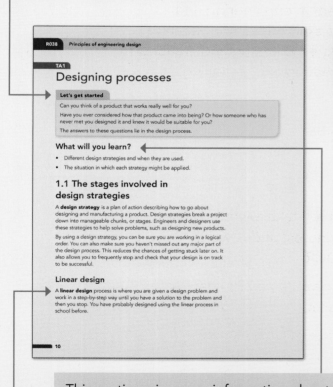

R038   Principles of engineering design

TA1

Designing processes

Let's get started

Can you think of a product that works really well for you?

Have you ever considered how that product came into being? Or how someone who has never met you designed it and knew it would be suitable for you?

The answers to these questions lie in the design process.

What will you learn?

- Different design strategies and when they are used.
- The situation in which each strategy might be applied.

1.1 The stages involved in design strategies

A **design strategy** is a plan of action describing how to go about designing and manufacturing a product. Design strategies break a project down into manageable chunks, or stages. Engineers and designers use these strategies to help solve problems, such as designing new products.

By using a design strategy, you can be sure you are working in a logical order. You can also make sure you haven't missed out any major part of the design process. This reduces the chances of getting stuck later on. It also allows you to frequently stop and check that your design is on track to be successful.

Linear design

A **linear design** process is where you are given a design problem and work in a step-by-step way until you have a solution to the problem and then you stop. You have probably designed using the linear process in school before.

10

This section gives you information about what content is covered in the topic.

Key words are highlighted in the text and explained fully in the glossary, often using examples, to ensure you fully understand key terminology.

Case study

Mobile phones

A mobile phone can contain between 300 and 1000 parts, made from over 70 different materials, including metals, composites, ceramics and polymers. Including the steps needed to make these parts, each phone has probably been through over 5000 manufacturing process steps! For example:

- The polymer casing is shaped by injection moulding.
- Lengths of wire are cut (wasted) for the antennae.

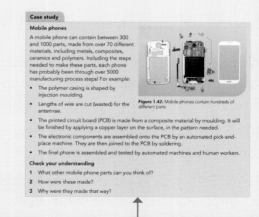

Figure 1.42: Mobile phones contain hundreds of different parts

- The printed circuit board (PCB) is made from a composite material by moulding. It will be finished by applying a copper layer on the surface, in the pattern needed.
- The electronic components are assembled onto the PCB by an automated pick-and-place machine. They are then joined to the PCB by soldering.
- The final phone is assembled and tested by automated machines and human workers.

Check your understanding

1 What other mobile phone parts can you think of?

2 How were these made?

3 Why were they made that way?

Case studies based on real-life situations put key concepts and practices into context. The accompanying questions check your understanding and challenge you to take your learning further.

How to use this book

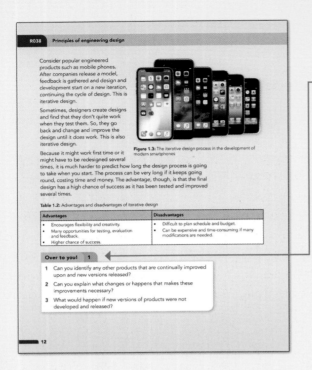

Over to you! activities let you apply your knowledge and think more deeply about your course.

Practical activities that you can do on your own give you the opportunity to practise important skills and techniques, and to prepare for your assessments.

Hands on! 1

1 Create a questionnaire to determine which computer game console is the most popular amongst your group/class. Ask a number of people and record the results.

2 Create a question to determine why they prefer their chosen console. Again, ask a number of people and record the results.

3 Which of these sets of answers would be easier to turn into a graph or diagram? Which one provides more information?

Stretch

Engineering designers use a variety of design strategies depending on the situation and who the solution must be suitable for. Some strategies include:

- user-centred design
- inclusive design
- ergonomic design.

Choose one of the design strategies. Explain how employing that design strategy would change the way you work and the decisions you would have to make during the design process.

Stretch activities and questions give you the opportunity to try more challenging questions and to extend your knowledge.

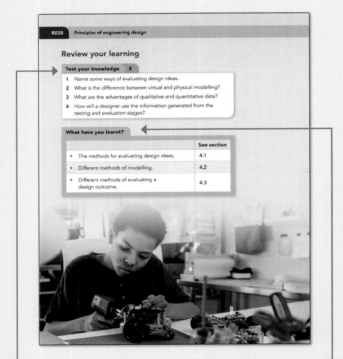

These question boxes give you regular opportunities to test your knowledge so that you feel ready for your exam or assessment.

Summary sections help you review your learning, to check you understand key concepts and can apply your learning. They also show you where to look back for more information if you need to read it again.

Support for you

Our resources in this series are designed to work together to help you with your Cambridge National course.

Your Student Book is where you will find the core information you need. This will help you with your knowledge and understanding of the subject. Information is arranged by unit and then by topic area, so you can easily find what you're looking for. Questions and activities will help you to apply your knowledge and understanding and to develop practical skills. You can assess your progress with the Test your knowledge questions. When you've completed the quiz, check your answers in the digital edition.

Your Revision Guide and Workbook supports you with the externally assessed unit of your course. The exam preparation section offers advice to help you get ready for this assessment. The Revision Guide section provides concise outlines of the core knowledge you need. Each page focuses on a small piece of learning to help you break your revision up into manageable chunks. The Workbook section brings your revision and learning together with practice questions. Digital quizzes help you to understand the language used in your assessment and to check your knowledge and understanding of key concepts. The Revision Guide and Workbook has not been through the OCR endorsement process.

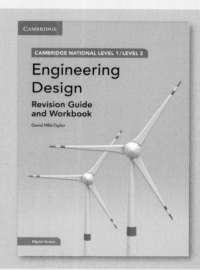

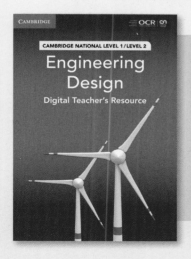

The Teacher's Resource is a rich bank of ideas to help your teacher create engaging lessons to meet the needs of your class. It contains PowerPoint slides, worksheets and links to external video content, in addition to activity and delivery ideas that can be personalised for your lessons. Digital quizzes help test understanding and unlock the language used in assessment.

R038 Principles of engineering design

Let's get started

Do you like to use logic and improvisation to solve problems? Do you like to let your imagination run wild?

Either working on their own or as part of a team, engineers design new things or make existing things better. From the latest in gaming entertainment to complex and life-saving medical equipment, engineers are at the heart of technological advancement.

What will you learn in this unit?

Whether you are aiming to become a designer or an engineer, you need to know about how products are designed and the different factors that influence their design, as well as how they are communicated, tested and evaluated. This will provide understanding that underpins the skills you will use in the other units of this course. In this unit, you will learn about the design process and all the stages that are involved.

In this unit you will learn about:

* different design strategies and when they are used **TA1**

* the stages of the iterative design process **TA1**

* types of criteria included in a design specification **TA2**

* how manufacturing and other considerations influence design **TA2**

* types of drawing used to communicate designs **TA3**

* methods of modelling and evaluating design ideas **TA4**.

How you will be assessed

This unit will be externally assessed by a one-hour 15-minute written exam that is worth 40% of your overall mark for this qualification. The exam includes two parts: a first section with ten multiple choice questions and a second section with short answer and extended response questions. In the exam, you will be expected to show that you understand this unit by answering questions about the design process and all of the stages that this involves.

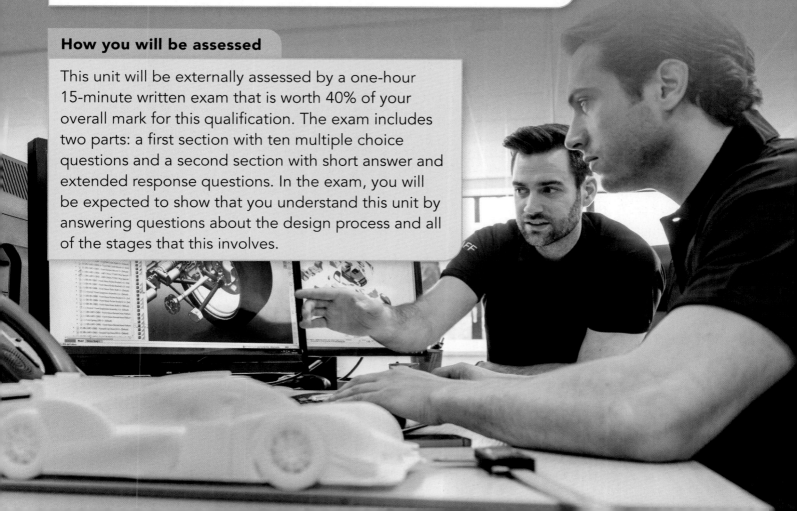

TA1

Designing processes

Let's get started

Can you think of a product that works really well for you?

Have you ever considered how that product came into being? Or how someone who has never met you designed it and knew it would be suitable for you?

The answers to these questions lie in the design process.

What will you learn?

• Different design strategies and when they are used.

• The situation in which each strategy might be applied.

1.1 The stages involved in design strategies

A **design strategy** is a plan of action describing how to go about designing and manufacturing a product. Design strategies break a project down into manageable chunks, or stages. Engineers and designers use these strategies to help solve problems, such as designing new products.

By using a design strategy, you can be sure you are working in a logical order. You can also make sure you haven't missed out any major part of the design process. This reduces the chances of getting stuck later on. It also allows you to frequently stop and check that your design is on track to be successful.

Linear design

A **linear design** process is where you are given a design problem and work in a step-by-step way until you have a solution to the problem and then you stop. You have probably designed using the linear process in school before.

Figure 1.1: The linear design process

There are advantages to linear design. Working in this way creates an easy plan to follow. You know which stage comes next and there aren't many difficult questions to answer. The disadvantage is that it doesn't allow you to modify or improve upon the design a great deal – you can't go back to designing or researching if your prototype doesn't work out. It also doesn't offer much chance to check that the design is going to be suitable until the end of the process.

Table 1.1: Advantages and disadvantages of linear design

Advantages	Disadvantages
• Plan is clear and easy to follow. • Each stage is completed thoroughly before moving on to the next.	• Lacks flexibility, so can stifle creativity and innovation. • Provides few opportunities to modify or improve design. • Difficult to check suitability of design until end of process.

Iterative design

Iterative design is a cyclic design process, which means the process of designing, testing and improving keeps going to produce new designs or developments (known as iterations) of the design. This can be done over and over until the best possible outcome is generated.

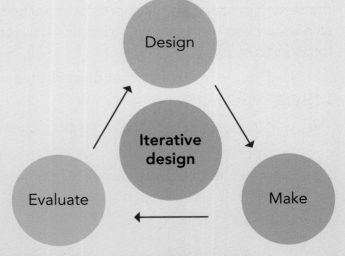

Figure 1.2: The iterative design process

Consider popular engineered products such as mobile phones. After companies release a model, feedback is gathered and design and development start on a new iteration, continuing the cycle of design. This is iterative design.

Sometimes, designers create designs and find that they don't quite work when they test them. So, they go back and change and improve the design until it *does* work. This is also iterative design.

Because it might work first time or it might have to be redesigned several times, it is much harder to predict how long the design process is going to take when you start. The process can be very long if it keeps going round, costing time and money. The advantage, though, is that the final design has a high chance of success as it has been tested and improved several times.

Figure 1.3: The iterative design process in the development of modern smartphones

Table 1.2: Advantages and disadvantages of iterative design

Advantages	Disadvantages
• Encourages flexibility and creativity. • Many opportunities for testing, evaluation and feedback. • Higher chance of success.	• Difficult to plan schedule and budget. • Can be expensive and time-consuming if many modifications are needed.

Over to you!   1

1   Can you identify any other products that are continually improved upon and new versions released?

2   Can you explain what changes or happens that makes these improvements necessary?

3   What would happen if new versions of products were not developed and released?

Inclusive design

Consider a lift in a shopping centre. It has been designed to be used by a wide range of people. It is large enough and strong enough for any person wishing to use it. It is often usable by wheelchair users and may have features such as braille on the buttons, or sounds that indicate that the doors are closing. Designing for as many people as possible is called **inclusive design**. When you design in this way you aim to create solutions that can be used by as many different people as possible. This means thinking about how to make your design accessible by considering the limitations some people may have, for example, due to their age or ability.

Figure 1.4: Braille markings and lights make lift buttons more accessible

User-centred design

Olympic cyclists have equipment that has been perfectly shaped, weighted and sized for them. It will have been manufactured with all of their personal preferences in mind. This is **user-centred design (UCD)**. To design this way, you have to start with the needs of the end user of the product. You base your research, designing and testing on that person and how they are going to use your product. You would do a lot of focus groups or interviews with the users and refer back to them regularly. For an Olympic cyclist, you might interview them to find out their preferences, show them the designs, get them to sit on and test the models until you have a final product. The final design might be unsuitable for most people, but perfect for them.

Figure 1.5: Some products are designed with just one person in mind

The advantage is this can make products very specialised for a small group of people or even a single individual. The disadvantage is that the improvements, and going back to the user, take time and money to accomplish – it is often a slow and expensive process.

Sustainable design

Sustainable design is an approach to creating products that considers and minimises environmental, social and economic impacts. To design in this way, you need to consider the impact making the product will have and the impact at the end of its life. When designing, you may think about **disassembly**, **reusability** and **longevity**.

Disassembly is taking the product apart easily. This makes recycling easier and more efficient. It also means you can change or repair parts. This can be as simple as being able to replace the batteries in a toy or as complicated as being able to swap an entire engine out of a car.

Figure 1.6: Reusable coffee cups reduce impact on the environment

Reusability is ensuring a product can be used over and over. For example, coffee cups made out of bioplastic can be reused many times. This creates less waste, which is better for the environment. Once it reaches the end of its usable life it may have a new function and be able to be used for something else.

Longevity is designing a product to be used for a long time. This means your customers don't dispose of it as quickly. This reduces both waste and the need for a new product. Takeaway food often comes with disposable forks and packaging that is designed to be used once then thrown away, requiring new packaging and cutlery for the next meal. This is often made worse by manufacturers using materials that are particularly harmful to the environment to save money.

Sustainable design also takes into account where the materials come from, where they go after, and how the labour is sourced. You might consider a sustainable approach if you were designing a product that was used in large quantities and frequently thrown away, such as plastic drinks straws. Some clients will be concerned about the environment as part of their mission statement and goals. Customers have also become increasingly aware of sustainability issues and may have strong opinions about the effect products have on the environment.

Ergonomic design

Imagine how frustrating it would be if the buttons on your games controller weren't where your fingers sat. Designing products while thinking about how we use them is called **ergonomic design**. To design in this way, you need to make your product a suitable size for the average user and consider what materials or textures they might find most comfortable. Designing in this way has the advantage that your product is easy and comfortable to use, reducing the chance of injury or strain.

Figure 1.7: Games controllers are designed to fit human hands comfortably

Advantages and disadvantages of design strategies

Table 1.3: Advantages and disadvantages of design strategies

Design strategy	Key features	Advantages and disadvantages
Inclusive design	Designing to be accessible to a large number of people	⊕ Usable by a large number of people
		⊖ Does not necessarily consider a wide range of abilities
		⊖ People with less common needs may be excluded by the design
User-centred design	Designing with end user and the working environment in mind	⊕ Optimises suitability for a specific group of people
		⊕ Maximises comfort, suitability and efficiency for that group
		⊖ Does not consider other groups of potential users
Sustainable design	Designing with environmental, social and economic impact in mind	⊕ Minimises impact on the environment and on people
		⊖ The most sustainable solution is not always the most efficient or cheapest solution
Ergonomic design	Designing using human measurements	⊕ Designs are comfortable, safe and easy to use
		⊖ Not always the most attractive or the cheapest design

Case study

Red Bull Racing team

Red Bull Racing has been making and racing Formula 1 cars since 2004. Formula 1 teams race cars that are as technologically advanced as possible. Any inefficient parts can make the difference between first and last place. This means that the engineers need to use the latest technologies and alter the car to include new technologies as they are invented. Each new advance means a new iteration of the car.

Continued

The Red Bull Racing car is made in assembly bays in Milton Keynes. More than 300 designers, aerodynamicists and machinists work on just one racing car. Each car has more than 6000 parts.

Each car is built with its specific driver in mind to support the driver through stresses, including heat build-up and g-force. The engineers will make the cockpit as ergonomic as possible – the seat shape and size, the distance to the pedals, and the steering wheels are all made to match the size, build and hand grip of the race driver. The car will also be balanced and designed with the weight of the specific driver in mind.

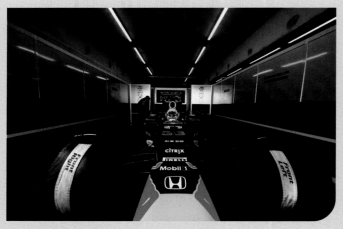

Figure 1.8: The Red Bull Racing car

And the designing doesn't stop there. During the course of a race season, the design team continually redesign and modify the car. By the end of just one race season it will have undergone 30 000 design changes. This takes into account new technology but also different track speeds, layouts and weather conditions.

Check your understanding

1   Identify who the Red Bull Racing team is designing for.

2   Explain why the design of the Formula 1 car can be considered an iterative design process.

3   Discuss how the Red Bull Racing team undertake user-centred design.

Stretch

Engineering designers use a variety of design strategies depending on the situation and who the solution must be suitable for. Some strategies include:

*   user-centred design
*   inclusive design
*   ergonomic design.

Choose one of the design strategies. Explain how employing that design strategy would change the way you work and the decisions you would have to make during the design process.

1.2 Stages of the iterative design process

Can you remember a time you tried something new and it didn't work first time? Given the choice to give up or try again, which did you do?

Iterative design answers the question 'what happens if a design misses the mark first time?'

Design

The design phase of iterative design is your chance to formulate a solution to a problem. This will usually involve you designing ideas to solve a problem a client has. Usually (but not always) this means designing a physical product.

Clients often need things designing that you may be unfamiliar with. You might be asked to design for people significantly older or younger than you, or with very different interests and preferences. So you must carry out research before you can start your designs.

Figure 1.9: The design phase

Analysis of the design brief

Your client will give you the **design brief**. This is a document explaining the requirements of the product to be designed. It will contain important information, including:

* what the product must do
* who the product is being designed for
* how long you have to design the product
* how much budget you have.

You will need to analyse the design brief. If your final product doesn't match it, it is not a success. Every point will need to be considered. You have to be clear what every point means. Ignoring the design brief means the product may not be suitable, or the design process will go over time or budget.

But remember – the client setting the brief is probably not an engineer. So, they might have a good idea about the budget, time constraints, **product requirements** and who their customers are, but they probably can't tell you about materials, manufacturing or technical details. You will need to do further research for them.

Figure 1.10: Interviewing the client can provide important insight into the design requirements

Methods of researching the product requirements

The design brief only tells you what the product must do to be successful. It doesn't tell you *how* to do it. To understand how to achieve the brief, you are going to have to do some research. Planning your research is important. You might need to track down documents, organise interviews or approach companies. All this takes time. Good research makes best use of your designing time, though, and gathers the information you need to make your design a success.

Types of information obtained from primary research

Primary research is information collected directly by you. You might look at existing products, interview experts, visit locations or produce questionnaires and surveys. Primary research is great because it is reliable: you know where the data came from and you know how it was collected. It is also the most up-to-date information you could hope for.

Table 1.4: Types of information obtained from primary research

Area of primary research	Example types of information you might obtain
Focus groups Interviews Surveys	• customers' opinions on products similar to the one you've been asked to design • what features they would expect on a product of this type • what sort of performance they would expect from a product like this
Observations	• what the customers' interests are • where they might use this product • what other products they own • fashions and trends that influence them
Product analysis	• how many similar products already exist • function and features of similar products • the price range of similar products
Industrial visits	• material availability that will limit the design options • machinery and processes available for manufacturing the product • expert opinions and insights

Hands on!   1

1 Create a questionnaire to determine which computer game console is the most popular amongst your group/class. Ask a number of people and record the results.

2 Create a question to determine why they prefer their chosen console. Again, ask a number of people and record the results.

3 Which of these sets of answers would be easier to turn into a graph or diagram? Which one provides more information?

Types of information obtained from secondary research

Secondary research is based on information that has been published elsewhere. You could look on the internet, or in books, magazines or publications. Secondary research quickly provides a lot of information, but you need to be careful reading and interpreting what it is saying. It won't help your product if you are repeating findings you found on the internet and don't know what they mean. You also have to be careful about the reliability of the data – has it come from a trustworthy source?

Table 1.5: Types of information obtained from secondary research

Area of secondary research	Example types of information you might obtain
Internet	• reviews on shopping sites for similar products • prices of similar products • online reviewers' opinions of similar products • guides and manuals for similar products from manufacturers' sites
Television programmes	• documentaries related to the product's history • television product review shows giving opinions on similar products • shopping and selling channels discussing the price and features of similar products
Databases	• numerical data relating to similar products, e.g. dimensions, success on the market, quantities currently on the market • data concerning material properties and costs
Textbooks	• scientific theory underpinning the type of product • guides to how components or similar products function • advances in technology that may concern the product type
Newspapers	• public perception surrounding the product type • moral issues concerning the type of product • social aspects that may affect the product

Over to you!   2

Think of three websites where you could research console game controllers.

1 What is the purpose of each of those sites?

2 What kinds of information could be found on those sites that might help you design a games controller?

Market research to determine existing products

Imagine you designed a great product and got it all the way to market only to find someone had already done the same thing... but better. To prevent this, one of the most valuable sources of research you can carry out is an existing product analysis. This means finding out as much as you can about existing products that are similar in function to the one you have been asked to develop. It's possible to do this through both primary and secondary research.

The advantage of researching existing products is that it gives you a good picture of the current cost, features and quality of similar products already on the market. You can use this to form a picture of what would be successful alongside these products.

Interviews with potential users and focus groups

A happy customer usually means a successful product. If you know who the likely users of your product are going to be, you can ask them questions to identify their preferences and what they would expect from your end product.

You need to carefully consider your questions to make sure the information you get is both relevant and useful to you. A question where they can express their feelings freely can be much more use than a 'yes' or 'no' answer. Similarly, asking them their eye colour is probably not going to help you reach a solution to your design problem.

Figure 1.11: Customer interviews provide important insight

Use of tables of anthropometric data

Take a look at the toothbrushes in Figure 1.12 – the handle on the child's toothbrush is shorter, thicker and more shaped than the adult one. When designing, you will need to research data relating to sizes. This size data is called **anthropometric** data. There are two main categories of anthropometric data: structural and functional.

Figure 1.12: A child's toothbrush and an adult's toothbrush

- **Structural anthropometry** relates to measurements when a body is in a still or fixed position, for example, the height or weight of a person or the size of their hand or head.

- **Functional anthropometry** relates to measurements with the body engaged in a task, for example, how far an arm can reach, or the length of a person's stride when walking.

Anthropometric data is collected by **anthropometrists** – scientists who take thousands of measurements of the human body. They put the data into tables for easy reference so you can use it when designing. These include the average sizes for a group of people, specific to an age range or gender group. If you were designing the child's toothbrush shown in Figure 1.12, for example, you might look up data about the dimensions of the hands of young girls and boys.

If you were to measure the hand size of 20 000 people and plot the results, the data would make a bell-shaped graph (see Figure 1.13). You may use charts like these to make sure your designs are a suitable size for most people. Engineers normally design to fit the 90% of people in the shaded area in the middle of the graph. By disregarding the left-hand 5% and the right-hand 5% (outside of the dotted lines on the graph) they remove the extremes and can design to encompass the greatest number of users.

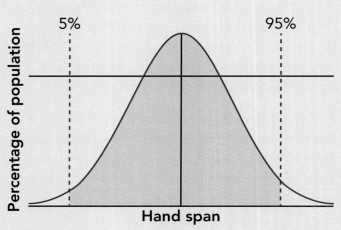

Figure 1.13: A normal distribution curve of hand size, showing the 5th–95th percentile

Ergonomics is when you use these measurements to help design a product. You can ensure it is going to fit correctly and be comfortable to use by checking the sizes in the anthropometric data and using them in your design.

If you were designing a computer workstation, as in Figure 1.14, you would need to make the chair and computer table the right height for the person using them. You would need to know the standing elbow height of the fifth percentile and the standing elbow height of the ninety-fifth percentile. Typically, a design should be comfortable to use for people between those heights.

An ergonomically designed product means less strain and injury for the person using it. A better experience will hopefully mean a more successful and popular product.

Figure 1.14: Typical use of data in an ergonomic design

Test your knowledge   1

1   What are the main differences between anthropometrics and ergonomics?

2   What are some key anthropometric measurements that could be used in the design of a bicycle.

3   Justify why designers might disregard the top and bottom fifth percentile of measurements.

Analysis of existing products

When researching, it helps to carefully analyse a product that is similar to the one you will be designing. It will provide clues to what works, what maybe doesn't work very well, and the expectations the customers might have of a product similar to yours. The objective here is for you to end up with an idea of how to create a product that is better than anything similar that is currently on the market.

ACCESS FM

To be thorough, it helps to have a strategy. Engineering students and designers often use the acronym **ACCESS FM** to help them analyse a competitor's product in depth. The acronym is easy to remember and gives you themes you can focus on. This makes sure you are asking the right questions to get useful information. Even better, if you are analysing more than one product, you will analyse them all in the same way, which makes your results fairer.

Table 1.6 explains what each letter of the acronym stands for and gives examples of questions that could be asked about a product. Table 1.7 uses the rucksack in Figure 1.15 to show how some of the questions could be answered. These examples should help guide you when completing your own ACCESS FM analysis.

Figure 1.15: A rucksack that a student might use for school or college

Table 1.6: Using ACCESS FM to analyse existing products

	Meaning	Example questions that could be asked
A	Aesthetics – consider what the product looks like	What does the product look like? What shapes have been used? What colours and textures have been used? Why? Does it follow a current theme or trend?
C	Cost – consider the cost of the product	Is this a typical price for this type of product? How has it been made affordable? How has it been made cost effective to make? Does the price of this product affect its popularity?
C	Customer – consider the customer that the product has been designed for	Who is the intended user for this product? How does the design suit their needs? What features have been included specifically for them?
E	Environment – consider how the product affects the environment	What is this product's impact on the environment? Is the product suitable for recycling? Are the materials sourced responsibly? Could it be disposed of safely?
S	Size – consider the dimensions of the product	How big is this product? Are its dimensions unusual for a product of this type? What proportions have been chosen in its design? Why?
S	Safety – consider safety concerns about the product	How has this product been designed to be safe? Does the product have safety guidance provided with it? Are there any laws or guidance covering this type of product?
F	Function – consider what the product does and how	What purpose does this product fulfil? How does it complete this purpose? Are there features that make this product superior to similar products?
M	Materials – consider the material choices that were made in the product	What materials have been used in the making of this product? Why have those materials been selected? Are the materials well suited for the function of this product?

Table 1.7: ACCESS FM analysis of a rucksack

ACCESS FM point	Analysis
Aesthetics	• This particular bag is plain blue; it is also available in other common block colours to appeal to a range of tastes. • The colour is bright to stand out which will help the bag be identified in a busy environment such as a school. • The simple, bold design is intended to be attractive to a wide group of people.
Cost	• The majority of the bag is made out of one type of synthetic polymer material, cutting down the need to source and transport a range of materials, ultimately reducing production costs. • The bag is unbranded, reducing associated licensing/copyright costs. This reduces the production costs but also affects the selling price.
Customer	• This is a generic multi-purpose bag but is primarily intended for students. • It has numerous pockets, padded straps for comfort and a sturdy construction making it suitable for this group of people. • The bag has a large capacity for carrying textbooks and devices.
Environment	• The plain design and simple aesthetic make it suitable for use in a range of different situations and places. • The size and shape are suitable for carrying numerous items, making the bag ideal for a school or college environment. • The waterproof material means it can be used in a variety of weather conditions. • The polymer material is possibly reusable. • As it is a thermoplastic, it could be recycled if it became damaged or was no longer required. • As the bag is made of one material, it is easily disposed of and does not require any complex disassembly.
Size	• The straps and dimensions have been designed for the height of a teenager or adult. • The square dimensions optimise space for schoolbooks. • The positioning of the zip allows a wide opening.
Safety	• The bag has no sharp edges due to its design and soft material. • The bag has sturdy, padded straps. These are attached securely to main rucksack and adjustable, reducing the chance of strain injury to the user. • Although there are no specific BSI standards or CE guides on this type of bag, it does follow guidelines on toxic materials, care instructions and general safety.
Function	• The bag's function is to transport personal belongings. It is designed to make this task easier by spreading the load across a person's back and shoulders. • The bag also has a hook so it can be hung from a peg.
Materials	• The bag is made from a synthetic polymer. The colour is bonded into the material so it won't run or wear off. • The polymer is also waterproof which provides some protection to the items inside. • There are some environmental concerns with the widespread use of plastics as they are mostly derived from fossil fuels.

Product disassembly

There is only so much you can tell from the outside of a product. Engineers will often take apart competitors' products to discover more about them. This is called disassembly.

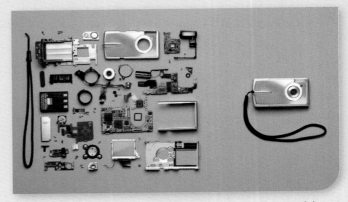

Figure 1.16: A camera before and after disassembly

- **Assembly methods:** When you take apart a product, it will give you clues about how it was assembled. You will discover whether temporary fixings, such as screws or clips, or more permanent methods, such as gluing or soldering, were used.

- **Materials used:** You will be able to look at the materials used more clearly. Different materials have different properties, so most products are not made from just one material. Metals are often used for strength and ductility when making fixings such as screws. Plastic is often used where complex shapes are required as it is easily shaped.

- **Production method:** When disassembling you can work out what method was used to make each part. This will require a bit of research and practice too. There is often more than one way to make each part, so the original engineer will have made decisions based on time, cost and suitability.

- **Component functions:** You can look at what each part does and how it contributes to the product as a whole. Sometimes, as with desktop computers, components are designed to be removed so you can upgrade them. The choice of components will have had a big effect on the overall cost of the product.

- **Maintenance concerns:** You can look at how each part is accessible to look after and repair. Most products need some level of cleaning and lubricating. In electronic products, batteries will often need to be accessed so they can be changed. In products with moving parts, parts may be accessible so they can be replaced. On a bike, for example, almost all parts are replaceable.

Hands on!   2

1   Can you find a product that is not designed to be taken apart and would have to be disposed of if a part went wrong?

2   Can you find any products around you that have been designed to be taken apart?

3   Can you name any of the temporary fixings used on these products to make that possible?

Production of an engineering design specification

Once you have done some research, you need to create a **design specification**. This is a list of things to address when designing but also acts as a check list to test the product against at the end. The easiest way to make this list is to partly base it on the design brief, but also include any new requirements that turned up when you analysed similar products, talked to the customers and did other research.

In Table 1.8, ACCESS FM has been used as a basis for starting to write specification points.

Table 1.8: Design specification for a hairdryer

A	Aesthetics	must use the client's brand logo and colour scheme
C	Cost	cost to manufacture, per unit, must be less than the typical hairdryer
C	Customer	should be particularly appealing to young adults aged 18–30
E	Environment	should be efficient in its use of electricity
S	Size	should weigh less than 600 g
S	Safety	must be safe to use temperature of exposed parts must not exceed 40 °C
F	Function	must dry wet hair in a reasonable time
M	Materials	must be made of insulating, heat-resistant materials

Sometimes, additional themes will be added, but the specification needs to be thorough and relevant to the product you are designing. The important points of a hairdryer, for example, include power settings and a required operating temperature. By contrast, specification points for a scooter might focus in greater detail on durability and weight.

When designing, you can use these points as a guide. After you have designed your product, these points can be used as a checklist to see if your design was successful.

Generation of design ideas by sketching

Some of the earliest known examples of engineering drawings date back to 2200 BCE. Today, sketching designs remains one of the quickest and most effective ways of recording your ideas. As an engineer, you will need to produce ideas that meet the points you identified in the specification. The development of a design often goes through several types of drawing.

Sketches

Designs often start as a **sketch** – a quick, inaccurate drawing designed to get a number of ideas down on paper quickly. Early sketches often don't use rulers or drawing tools and are more concerned about the 'feel' of the idea. As technology develops, it is becoming more common for sketches to be done using digital devices which allow for easier editing, duplicating and adding quick, effective colour and shading.

Technical drawings

As the ideas develop, you will start to add more detail, for example, considering size, scale and material considerations. Drawings displaying this data are called technical drawings and can be hand drawn or computer generated. There are many kinds of technical drawing, each with its own purpose and rules on how to draw it.

Presentation drawings

Presentation drawings aim to convey as much information about a design as possible. They may contain a mix of realistic drawings, technical drawings and computer generated designs. They will also aim to contain all the specific data that is needed to produce a product. These drawings are often presented to a client or manufacturer to convey information about the final product.

Generation of design ideas by modelling

Modelling a product in the later stages of design allows it to be manipulated and handled. Early **models** are often smaller than life size, made from easily worked modelling materials such as card, paper and foam. More thorough and detailed models are made to enable testing.

Make and evaluate

Creating models of your design is only the start of the story. The models you produce can be used to check that the design is suitable and is going to meet your client's brief. Engineers will use the tests as a way of gathering evidence and proving the product is fit for purpose. As such, a range of different models of the design will have to be made with different aims in mind.

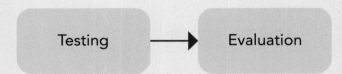

Figure 1.17: The evaluate phase

The reasons for the use of modelling

Often, setting up the machinery and equipment required to make a product is very expensive, complex and time-consuming. Even a simple product, such as a hand torch (see Figure 1.18), needs a lot of component parts.

Every part needs setting up, making and finishing – more than 30 individual steps. The manufacturer will need to set up a workspace with machines, prepare moulds or jigs, and train staff to make each of these steps possible.

To ensure a design is going to be suitable before investing a lot of time and money, engineers produce models. Models enable tests for a range of reasons, including to test proportions, scale and function.

Using modelling to test proportions

You've drawn some design ideas and you think your product looks great. Can you be sure it still looks good when you turn it? Does it look good from the top? What about far away or up close? Models can be made to test the shape and overall look of the product and answer questions like this. You can view a model from every angle and then return to your designs to make sure they are perfect.

Using modelling to test scale

You've probably done research to identify the best dimensions for your product and have a general idea that it's the right size. Modelling the product to scale, however, allows you to interact with it and be sure your product dimensions are going to work. When designing a hand torch (see Figure 1.18) you might need to check that the electronic components and batteries will fit inside it. You also need to check the handle is going to be a suitable size for the user's hand. You might also want to check the torch will fit inside a tool box or a pocket.

Figure 1.18: A hand torch is a simple product but is made up of many components

Figure 1.19: 3D models can be viewed from any angle

Figure 1.20: Scale is important, especially where the object must interact with other things

Using modelling to test function

Models can be made to test function – in other words, the way a product is going to work. This could be any aspect of the product's functionality. When designing a hand torch, for example, you could model the way the torch switches on or how it opens up when you need to change the batteries; you could also model the circuit designed to go into the torch. When you make a model to test function it doesn't necessarily have to look like the final product (though it can). It just needs to simulate the mechanism that will be used. These feasibility prototypes will show if your product will physically work and might also highlight problems or risks in its operation that hadn't occurred to you on paper.

Virtual modelling of the design idea

Virtual modelling is using a computer program to create a computer model of your design in three dimensions. It is relatively quick and inexpensive. Colour, shading and lighting can be added to increase realism.

Figure 1.21: Virtual modelling is often used to visualise concept cars

- Virtual models can be altered quickly and easily. Errors can be undone instantly and modifications can be made without restarting, saving time and money. This means you can experiment with the design without worrying about starting again or making an error. You can also quickly try out a range of variations on your design and still have the original if you are not completely sure of your design choice.

- Virtual models can be shared very easily. Designs can be shared and explored by the client, other designers, experts or customers to get feedback. Engineers can also work remotely on digital designs, allowing designers around the world to work collaboratively. Having a digital copy of the design is also useful when you want to create a new iteration of the design or use components again for a similar product.

- Virtual models can also be tested in a **simulation**. Engineers working on products can use computer simulations to test them in different situations. Models with moving parts can be tested to see if the parts move correctly. Models can be force- or pressure-tested to see if they break or if they have weak points. Products that need to be aerodynamic, such as planes and cars, can be tested to see how the air flows around them. These tests are often quicker and cheaper to do than creating a physical model.

Physical modelling of the design idea

Physical modelling is creating a real model of your design and still has an important place in the modern design process. Physical models allow a level of interaction that drawings and virtual models don't. A client or customer will usually get the best understanding of your idea by picking up and exploring a model of the design.

Figure 1.22: A scale model of a wind turbine

Physical models tend to be quick and cheap. They can be made from simple modelling materials when testing scale and proportions. Teams of designers often make card models before committing to a design. They use this method because it is cheap and fast, requiring simple tools to work.

Physical models can be made using rapid prototyping. The developed model of the component in Figure 1.23 has been 3D printed. While 3D printing remains too slow to manufacture a lot of products comercially, it allows the digital model of a design to be converted into a physical model. This gives a physical model all of the advantages of the digital model described previously, for example, it is detailed, accurate and easily altered and adjusted.

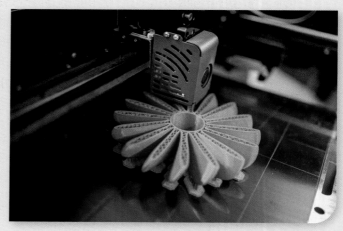

Figure 1.23: The developed model of this component has been 3D printed

Physical models can undergo a wide variety of tests. Tests allow you to gather supporting data to show how successful the design is. Tests can also highlight areas of your design that need addressing before you can call it complete. Some common tests include usability, focus group, non-destructive and destructive.

Usability testing: Using the model in the environment it was intended for. This tells you if your design works and if it works well.

Focus group testing: Using the model to show to a focus group. This provides useful feedback about whether or not the customer will like your final design and any alterations that would make it more appealing.

Non-destructive testing: Testing the limitations of your model without causing it damage. This might involve tests such as visual inspection, radiography or using water to check it for leaks. Non-destructive tests can identify flaws and weak points in your design.

Destructive testing: Testing your model until it breaks. This is often used to check safety. Tests might include crushing, dropping, submerging or setting the model on fire. This will identify if there are safety concerns regarding your product so that you can ensure it meets legal safety standards.

Test your knowledge 2

1 Identify two tests a model might be built for.

2 How might making a model improve the design of a product?

3 What are the advantages of a virtual model compared to a physical model?

Manufacture or modification of the prototype

Once your product has been tested, you need to decide if it requires further modification. Because this is an iterative design cycle, if there are improvements to make, you can go back to the design stage and make them, create a new model and test again. If there are no modifications to make, the design process is finished.

Comparison of the model or prototype against the requirements of the design brief and specification

There are two main areas to evaluate your model against to ensure it is successful: the design brief and the design specification.

The design brief: Does your design do what the client asked? The client presented you with an initial problem to solve. Even if you think your product is amazing, it still needs to meet the design brief.

A product that doesn't complete the required function, isn't suitable for the client's target audience, went over time or budget or isn't in keeping with the ethos of the company will be a failure and you will need to revisit your product design.

The design specification: Does your design meet the success criteria of the specification you wrote? Using your research, you identified specific details that your design needed to include. You can evaluate your design against these points, using them as a checklist. As before, if any points are not met, it is your duty to revisit the design and see if a modification can be made.

Case study

The Dyson vacuum cleaner

There is an increasing trend of low cost home electricals that sacrifice quality in material choice or manufacture method in order to be cheaper than their competitors. James Dyson's vacuum cleaner aimed to ignore this trend, instead relying on highlighting his superior engineered design to make sales.

James Dyson is famously reputed to have produced 5127 **prototype** models to improve his design, one small step at a

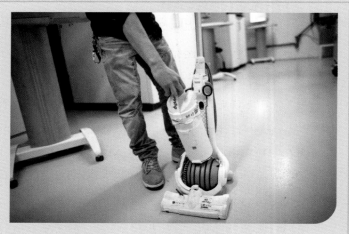

Figure 1.24: A Dyson vacuum cleaner

time. Dyson was an independent designer with a small budget to work with. For these prototypes, he often used foam and card which reduced the modelling cost but the time these models took meant he had to rely on his wife for financial support.

By persevering with the iterative design process – modelling and testing new ways of making a vacuum cleaner work – he created a product that had many advantages over the products already on sale.

Today, Dyson is a large manufacturer. It has developed hairdryers, fans and washing machines using the same principle. Dyson design teams continue to model and test new ideas, often in card and foam, creating designs that work in new and innovative ways.

This design approach means customers have an expectation of good quality and are often very loyal to the brand.

Continued

Check your understanding

1   Explain the problem associated with a long design and modelling process.

2   Justify how using iterative design and testing has resulted in the Dyson company being associated with quality.

3   Consider *two* tests that might have been done by Dyson on his prototypes.

Review your learning

Test your knowledge   3

1   What are the features of an iterative design process?

2   Explain the difference between primary and secondary research, giving the advantages of each.

3   What are the advantages of modelling a design idea?

4   Why would an engineer use a design process in developing new design ideas?

What have you learnt?

	See section
• A range of design strategies.	1.1
• The features of these design strategies and when they are used.	1.1
• The order, content and purpose of each stage of the iterative design process.	1.2

Design requirements

Let's get started

Have you ever wondered how some products become known as the best in their field? Have you considered how designers make sure their product will cover all of the many areas?

What will you learn?

- Types of criteria included in a design specification.
- How manufacturing and other considerations influence design.

2.1 Types of criteria included in an engineering design specification

There can be many different requirements in a design specification. As well as being used for product analysis, ACCESS FM can be used as a framework to check that a variety of different requirements are included. Some of these criteria consider the requirements of the user or customer, while others consider the requirements of the manufacturer, as shown in Table 1.9.

Table 1.9: Examples of criteria included in a design specification

ACCESS FM category		Example of requirement	Main source of requirement
A	Aesthetics	What colour(s) the product should be	User
		What texture the surface should have	User
		What the product smells like	User
		What the product tastes like	User
		What noise the product makes	User
C	Cost	How much the customer pays for the product	User
		How much the product costs to make	Manufacturer
C	Customer	Who will buy the product	User (Customer)
		Who will use the product	User
		Who else might be affected by the product	User
E	Environment	How much recycled material is used in the product	Manufacturer and customer
		Should it be possible to recycle the product after use	Manufacturer and customer
		Can the product be repaired rather than replaced	Manufacturer and user
		What packaging should be used for the product	Manufacturer
S	Size	What size the product should be (e.g. maximum length, height, width)	User
		How much the product should weigh	User
S	Safety	What safety features are needed in the product	Manufacturer and user
		What standards and regulations must the product meet	Manufacturer
F	Function	How the product will perform the task it is needed for	Manufacturer and user
		Where it will be used	User
		How it should be tested (and how well it will have to perform during testing)	Manufacturer
		What instructions are needed to use the product	User
		What maintenance will be needed in use	User
M	Materials	What quantity of products are to be made	Manufacturer
		What processes must be used to make the product	Manufacturer
		What materials are available/must be used to make the product	Manufacturer

Needs and wants

The criteria in a design specification can be divided into two types: **needs** and **wants**.

Needs are characteristics that the product *must* have. If any needs are not achieved, the product will not do what it is required to do.

For example, a specification for a bicycle might include: 'it must be able to support a rider weighing up to 100 kg'. This is a need – if the bicycle cannot support the rider, it will break and cannot be ridden.

Wants are characteristics that the user or designer *would like* the product to have. Wants may help a product to be successful, but they are not essential for the product to do what it is required to do.

For example, a specification for a bicycle might include: *'the frame should be red in colour'*. This is a want – even if the bicycle is a different colour, it could still be ridden.

Figure 1.25: What might be included in the specification of this bicycle?

Quantitative and qualitative criteria

Each criteria in a design specification can be classified as **quantitative** or **qualitative**.

Quantitative criteria are **objective** and can be measured. For example, *'the handlebar on the bicycle must have a diameter of 15 ± 1 mm'*. An advantage of quantitative criteria is that objective measurements can be made. This means that the measurement is against a commonly accepted **standard** or value, such as length in metres or weight in grams. Quantitative points are sometimes easier to work with, because they have a definite value and a right and wrong. They can easily be proved to be successful by measuring the final product – if the handlebars in Figure 1.25 are made and measured to be too big or small, the product is a failure. There is no grey area or judgement to be made.

Qualitative criteria are **subjective**. This means that they are judged based on the opinion of the assessor. Different assessors may have different opinions. For example, for a specification point that states *'the handlebar on the bicycle must be comfortable to hold'* one assessor may agree, another may disagree. This can make them harder to achieve. For products that are to be made in large quantities, qualitative assessment may involve market research asking many users their opinion, to establish the judgement of the majority.

Test your knowledge   1

1   Explain the difference between needs and wants.

2   What are the differences between quantitative and qualitative criteria on a design specification?

3   Why might a designer prefer to use a design specification that mainly contains quantitative criteria?

Reasons for the product criteria included in the design specification (ACCESS FM)

Using ACCESS FM keeps our specification relevant to information we need to design the product. As when we used it to analyse competitor products, it means we have considered a wide range of important points. Each of these points is included for a purpose.

Aesthetics

Aesthetics are important as the product has to appeal to the customer. For example, a toy rattle for a baby may be brightly coloured as saturated colours are easier for young eyes to see.

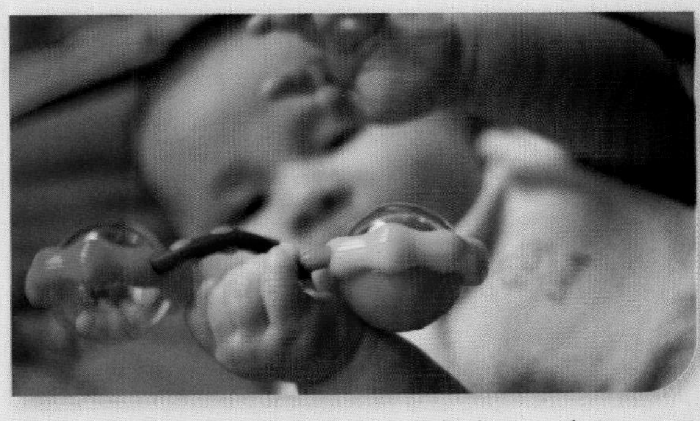

Figure 1.26: Why do you think the rattle is colourful?

Cost

If the product costs too much, customers will not buy it. If it is too expensive to make, the manufacturer will not be able to make any profit from the product, so will not want to make it. The cost constraints will likely have an effect on material choice, manufacturing method and even the time taken to design the product.

Customer

Defining the customer in the specification makes sure the product is suitable for them and increases the chance of success.

The designer also needs to know if the customer and the user of the product are the same person. For example, the baby's rattle has to appeal to the adults that buy it but also must be a suitable size for the babies to use. If it was designed to be ergonomic for the buyer to hold and shake, it would be too big and heavy for a baby!

Environment

Customers may avoid a product if it is not environmentally friendly. There are also environmental laws which stop or limit manufacturers using some materials, products and designs.

Some companies have goals relating to their environmental impact. Any product they require will have to reflect these ideals.

Size

Specification points relating to size might relate to how the product interacts with other items. The manufacturer may only have certain processes or materials available to make the product. These may limit the size of the product. The choice of materials may also be limited by the properties needed for the product to perform its function.

Safety

Safety considerations are often included as specification points. This is because an unsafe or dangerous product cannot be used. For example, the baby's rattle must not be made from a toxic material or have any small parts or sharp edges that could cause injury.

Function

The user may also have requirements for how the product functions. For example, for the rattle it needs to make a sound when shaken, but not be too loud! There may also be requirements for certain features – design choices that set the product aside from competitors.

Materials

There may be product requirements that relate directly to the choice of materials. Different materials have very different properties and are processed in different ways.

Hands on!

Look at the chair you are sitting on.

1 Write out a list of the design criteria that you think the designer used. What are the reasons for each of these criteria?

2 Identify which of these criteria are needs and which are wants.

3 Identify which of these criteria could be quantitative. What would appropriate values for these criteria be?

Test your knowledge   2

1 Explain why a design specification normally includes aesthetic criteria.

2 Explain why a manufacturer would want environmental criteria included in a design specification.

3 Give three details about the customer which may be included in a design specification. How would a designer use each of these pieces of information?

2.2 How manufacturing considerations affect design

When an engineer is designing a product, some criteria in the design specification will directly affect how the product will be made. These include:

- the quantity of parts to be made
- the materials that are to be used and the forms in which these are available
- the processes and equipment that will be used to make the product.

These requirements also affect each other and the design of the product. As you are designing you will need to think about:

- what materials are most suitable
- how you might shape those materials to create the product.

Scale of manufacture

The **scale of manufacture** refers to the number of copies of an identical product that need to be manufactured at one time.

One-off

One-off production involves making one product at a time. This could be a prototype or a product made for a specific customer, such as a tailor-made jacket, a crane for a large construction project, or a satellite.

Figure 1.27: One-off production of a handbag

In one-off production, the processes and machines are used to make many different products. The design can be varied massively between these products. This means that the equipment must be able to switch between different designs. This typically means that the machines are controlled by skilled human workers. Labour costs per product are high but capital costs can be low, especially where they are using equipment they already have.

Batch

Batch production is where identical products are made together in groups. Most products sold in high street stores, such as clothes or furniture, are made in batches. The size or appearance can be changed between different batches.

In batch production, the equipment is used to make the same product again and again. The product design should mean that every part has very little variation, so computers can control machining operations, repeating the same tasks over and over again. The labour cost per product is low. Although the cost of the computer-controlled equipment and the cost of writing the code to control the machines is high, when this is divided between all the products to be made, the capital costs per product can be low.

Mass

Mass production is where large quantities of identical products are made, with the same product being made over and over again. Cars and nuts and bolts are mass produced, typically on a production line.

Mass production often uses a mix of manually- and computer-controlled processes. It will also use templates, moulds and work holding devices, such as jigs and fixtures. These help to reduce the labour time to mark out products, reducing the labour costs per product.

Figure 1.28: Robots welding cars on a production line

Comparing scales of production

Table 1.10: Characteristics of different scales of manufacture

Typical characteristic	One-off production	Batch production	Mass production
Labour cost per product	highest	⟵	lowest
Level of worker skill	highest	⟵	lowest
Level of automation	lowest	⟶	highest
Cost of equipment	lowest	⟶	highest
Capital cost per product	highest	⟵	lowest
Total cost of making, per product	highest	⟵	lowest
Number of products made per time period	lowest	⟶	highest

Material availability and form

The main factor determining which material will be used is normally the combination of properties required by the product.

Most materials are available in a wide range of different shapes, sizes or **stock forms** (see Figure 1.29). Each requires different processing methods, which affects the cost.

Metals

Metals are available in a wide range of solid forms, including the stock forms shown in Figure 1.29. They are processed into ingots that are then melted down into stock shapes, a process requiring very high temperatures. Metals are usually denser and more malleable than other materials. Many metals are costly due to their relative rarity and costs involved in processing them.

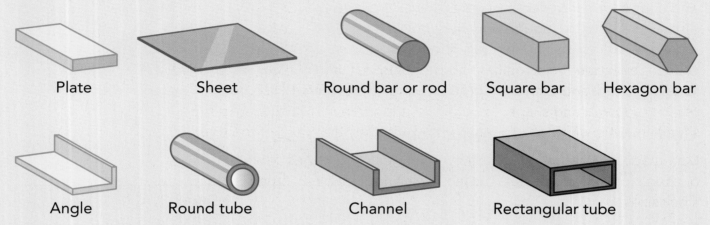

| Plate | Sheet | Round bar or rod | Square bar | Hexagon bar |

| Angle | Round tube | Channel | Rectangular tube |

Figure 1.29: Common stock forms of materials

An **alloy** is a mixture of two or more metals or other elements such as carbon, which have enhanced properties compared to single metals. Brass is an alloy made from copper and zinc. It is harder and is easier to work on a machine than pure copper. **Ferrous metals** are metals or alloys which contain iron. Ferrous metal alloys are often mixed with different proportions of carbon which change their properties. Stainless steel is a ferrous alloy containing carbon (<1.0%) and chromium (<11.5%). It is more resistant to corrosion than iron. **Non-ferrous metals** or alloys do not contain iron. Brass and bronze are common non-ferrous alloys.

Plastics

Plastics (also known as polymers) are available in a range of different forms, depending on whether the plastic is a thermoplastic polymer (formed by heat and can be reformed or reused) or a thermosetting polymer (formed by permanent chemical reactions and cannot be reused).

Thermoplastics are processed into pellets which can then be cast or extruded. Because they can be reheated and shaped, thermoplastic polymers are available from manufacturers in most of the stock form shapes that metals come in. Plastics also have the advantage of being pre-coloured, patterned, textured or even transparent.

Thermosetting polymers can only be shaped (or cast) once. The raw form of thermosetting polymers is available either as a powdered mix that requires heat and pressure to start the chemical reaction, or as two-part liquids that must be mixed to start the reaction (as for epoxy glue). This means the manufacturer usually forms the mix directly into the shape that is needed for the final product.

Wood

Wood is available in natural or man-made forms. Natural wood is seasoned (carefully dried) and then shaped by wasting. It is available in square sections, dowels and shaped mouldings. It is also available in planks and sheets, but the width of a sheet is often limited by the width of the tree.

Man-made boards are produced by gluing either particles of wood or sheets of wood together. These sheets are available in much larger stock sizes.

Designers will often modify their designs so that they can use a stock form of material – this is normally much cheaper than having a material made specially to the form needed, even if it means having to join different parts together. They will also try to use a standard size to reduce the amount of material that has to be cut away. This both saves money and reduces environmental impact, by reducing waste.

Over to you!   1

Look at all the products in the room around you.

1   Identify which products are made from stock forms of material.

2   How has the use of stock forms of material affected their design?

Types of manufacturing processes

Manufacturing processes change the shape, size or properties of a product in a useful way. There are six different types of manufacturing process, each of which change materials or products in a different way.

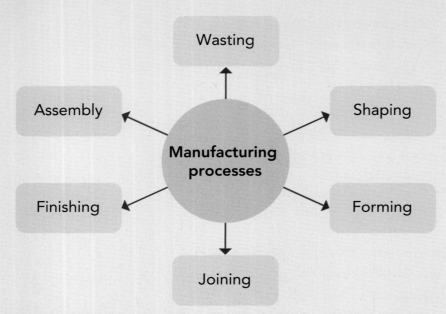

Figure 1.30: Types of manufacturing processes

For each type of process, there may be several different methods or tools that could carry it out.

Wasting

Many manufacturing operations start with a piece of material larger than the part being manufactured. Tools or machines are used to remove the material that is not needed in the form of the part being made.

Wasting processes remove material (see Figure 1.31). Often this involves either cutting or chipping away material using a tool with a sharp edge or melting material at the point where it needs to be separated. After wasting there will be a smaller quantity of material left in the product. The material that is removed is normally scrap or waste.

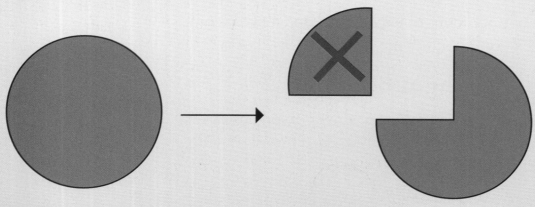

Figure 1.31: Wasting

To make a complicated shape it might take several process steps, as each feature will have to be wasted separately. This can be very time-consuming and costly. When designing products, designers will often try to minimise the need for wasting processes by using standard forms of material.

Table 1.11: Examples of wasting processes

Material	Wasting processes
Metals	milling
Metals and polymers	shearing
Metals, polymers ceramics and wood	routing
	laser-cutting
	sawing
	filing
	threading
	turning

Figure 1.32: Using a file to remove material from a metal workpiece held in a bench vice

Shaping

Shaping processes involve a change of state of the material (see Figure 1.33). This means that the material changes from being a solid to a liquid, or from being a liquid to a solid. For example, a material might be heated until it melts, then poured into a mould. As it cools it solidifies into its new shape. A big advantage of shaping is that a complicated 3D shape can be made in a single process step, with very little waste.

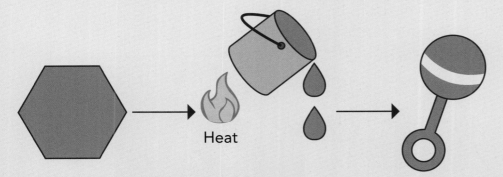
Heat

Figure 1.33: Shaping

Most shaping processes, except 3D printing, require some form of mould. Some processes, such as for the sand casting of metals, use moulds that are destroyed to remove the product. Processes such as the die casting of metals and injection moulding of polymers use metal moulds. These can be very expensive to manufacture, so are typically reused many times. However, in these cases the product design must include no features that would trap the product inside the mould, such as overhanging edges.

Figure 1.34: Carbide lathe inserts are made by powder metallurgy

Table 1.12: Examples of shaping processes

Material	Shaping process
Metals	sand casting
	die casting
Polymers	injection moulding
	3D printing
Ceramics	powder metallurgy

Forming

Forming involves changing the shape of the material without a change of state (see Figure 1.35). This includes processes that bend or deform sheets of material. Many forming processes heat the material to make it easier to change its shape, but the material never reaches its melting point. Normally, no material is lost during the forming process.

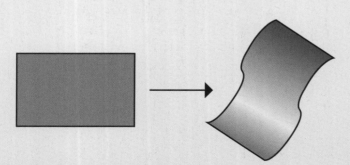

Figure 1.35: Forming

Figure 1.36: Sheet metal blanks are formed into simple folded panels or boxes using a general-purpose block and blade tool on a forming press

Forming processes limit design choices as they can only make simple shapes, with no overhanging features. They are often followed by wasting processes, to remove excess material from around the formed shape.

Table 1.13: Examples of forming processes

Material	Forming process
Metals	forging
	press forming
Polymers	strip heating
	vacuum forming
Ceramics	moulding

Joining

Many components are made from more than one piece or type of material. This could be because it is difficult to manufacture the size or shape needed from a single piece of material, or that different types of materials are needed in the product with different properties. For example, a safety helmet needs a hard outer shell but an inside lining that is comfortable for the user.

Joining processes are used to attach separate pieces of material together to make products (see Figure 1.37). Joining processes can be divided into two types: permanent and temporary. Permanent joints can only be taken apart by breaking the material. Temporary joints can be removed without damaging the material. For example, the maintenance hatch on a machine would be attached by screws (temporary joint) rather than being glued (permanent joint), as engineers may need to open the hatch if the machine needs to be repaired or serviced.

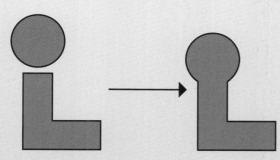

Figure 1.37: Joining

Figure 1.38: Using a rivet gun to attach a gunwale to a river canoe

When using joining processes, designers have to take into account that the properties of the joint may be different from the rest of the material.

Table 1.14: Examples of joining processes

Material	Joining process
Metals	soldering
	brazing
	welding
	press forming
Polymers and wood	rivets
	mechanical fasteners (screws, nuts and bolts)

Finishing

Finishing processes change the surface of the material in a useful way (see Figure 1.39). For example, they may change the colour, to make the product look more attractive to a user, or they may make the product perform better or longer when in use.

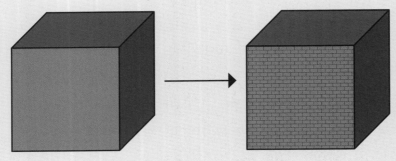

Figure 1.39: Finishing

Figure 1.40: Fine polymer powders are applied electrostatically before being cured in a baking oven

Many finishing processes are additive. They involve depositing a layer of another material with different properties. An advantage of this is that rather than making a whole product from an expensive material, this might allow a product to be made from a cheaper material with lower (or different) properties. This can then be finished by applying a layer of a more expensive material to achieve the surface properties needed.

Table 1.15: Examples of finishing processes

Material	Finishing process
Metals	electroplating
	powder coating
Polymers, ceramics and wood	painting (brush, spray), varnishing

Assembly

Most products are made from more than one part. **Assembly** is the process of fitting these parts together. This can involve some joining processes, such as soldering or the use of screws, as well as aligning, mating, pushing or sliding parts together.

Figure 1.41: Engineer assembling car doors in car factory

When designing parts to be assembled, features such as edges and holes must line up. This is normally controlled by stating a **tolerance** for each dimension on the design – this is the maximum that the dimension is allowed to vary from the target value.

Production costs

A main reason why manufacturing considerations affect the design is the **production costs**. Manufacturers need to make products at a cost where they can sell them for a profit.

There may be several different ways of making a product. The manufacturer will need to choose which of these can make the product most effectively and at a suitable cost. The main contributors to cost are labour costs, capital costs, overheads and materials.

Labour costs

Labour costs are based on how long it takes to make each product and how much the workers are paid for their time. These costs are higher if you want to manufacture more products because they will take more time and more people to achieve.

Capital costs

Capital costs are the one-time expenses you need to get the product manufacturing process up and running. They include the cost of the factory, the machinery and the land. Because they are one-off expenses, if you bought a factory to make just one product, the cost of that product would have to include the cost of your factory! If you made thousands of products, these costs would be split between all of the products. In effect, the more products made, the cheaper the capital costs per product.

Overheads

Overheads are the general costs of running the manufacturer's factory. They might include rent, rates and heating for the factory. Insuring and powering the machines is also an expense. For example, working with metal usually requires a lot of heat and this cost needs to be considered in the cost of manufacturing the final product.

Materials

Manufacturers also need to purchase materials. Several factors affect the cost of a material before it even gets to the factory.

- **Availability** If it is readily available a material is generally more affordable. Materials in short supply and in high demand, such as gold, are more expensive because people are willing to pay more for them. These materials are considered rare.

- **Location** If the materials must be transported large distances, this creates a transportation cost.

When you are designing, you will consider which process manufacturers are likely to choose to make each component of your design. One of the main factors that will interest your client is the total cost of the labour and capital per product. A product that is too expensive to produce would not be considered a success and would have to go back to the design stage.

Case study

Mobile phones

A mobile phone can contain between 300 and 1000 parts, made from over 70 different materials, including metals, composites, ceramics and polymers. Including the steps needed to make these parts, each phone has probably been through over 5000 manufacturing process steps! For example:

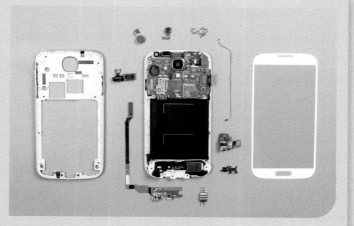

Figure 1.42: Mobile phones contain hundreds of different parts

- The polymer casing is shaped by injection moulding.

- Lengths of wire are cut (wasted) for the antennae.

- The printed circuit board (PCB) is made from a composite material by moulding. It will be finished by applying a copper layer on the surface, in the pattern needed.

- The electronic components are assembled onto the PCB by an automated pick-and-place machine. They are then joined to the PCB by soldering.

- The final phone is assembled and tested by automated machines and human workers.

Check your understanding

1 What other mobile phone parts can you think of?

2 How were these made?

3 Why were they made that way?

Over to you!   2

Choose a product that you are familiar with that is made from metal.

1 Identify all of the processes that were used to make this product.

2 Why were these processes used rather than the alternatives?

2.3 Influences on engineering product design

Market pull and technology push

Market pull begins with a person or group of people with a perceived need. A group of people will have a particular problem and there isn't a product out there that solves that problem. A good example of market pull was the need for digital cameras. Old film cameras were bulky and required reels of film that took time to develop and couldn't hold a lot of pictures. People demanded a simpler and more advanced way to store photos. Eventually this led to the development of the digital camera, as technology caught up with this demand.

Figure 1.43: Digital cameras were developed because people wanted to take lots of photos and view them immediately

Technology push begins with a technological breakthrough. A company will innovate a new way of doing something or a whole new product and will market it in the belief people might want it. A good example of technology push was the touch screen. Touch screens were invented in the 1960s but only became popular much later on when they were used in computers in the 1980s. Now they can be found in all sorts of everyday devices.

Figure 1.44: Touch screens were invented in 1965 but only became popular once the technology had been refined

British and International Standards

Designers must ensure that their products comply with certain standards in order for them to be safe and marketable. The standards vary depending on the type of product and where it is going to be sold. Markings are used to identify products that are deemed to meet these standards.

Table 1.16: Standards and their marks

	British Standards are produced by the British Standards Institution (BSI). Products must meet a range of quality checks through testing to become certified to these standards. Certain products that are found to meet criteria for quality and accuracy can bear the BSI Kitemark logo. BSI marks are used in the UK but are recognised and respected internationally. They give customers assurance of quality and safety.
	The CE marking is used on products throughout Europe. To hold it, products must meet a range of standards, usually related to safety. A product bearing the CE mark indicates that it has been assessed by the manufacturer and deemed to meet EU safety, health and environmental protection requirements. It is required for products manufactured anywhere in the world that are then going to be marketed in the EU.
	The UKCA (United Kingdom Conformity Assessed) marking came into effect on 1 January 2021. It was designed to replace the CE mark in the UK and is the new UK product marking for products being sold in Great Britain (England, Scotland and Wales). It will not be recognised in the EU market. Products that have to meet European requirements will still need the CE marking to be sold in the EU.
	International Standards are created by the International Organization for Standardization (ISO). They develop standards to make sure that products are good quality, safe and efficient. A manufacturer can pay for a third party to test a product and confirm it meets the relevant standards, allowing it to bear an ISO mark.
	The Lion Mark is a British symbol brought into use in 1988. A product with the Lion Mark has been tested and meets EN 71 and EN 62115, both of which are European toy safety standards. Tests include flammability and toxicity. It is not mandatory for all toys to bear the Lion Mark but it is intended to give the customer confidence in a product's safety and suitability.
	Brought into widespread use in 1995, this mark is used to warn that a product is not suitable for children under 3 years of age. It means the product represents a health and safety concern for very young children, often because it contains small, sharp or toxic parts. The nature of the hazard is usually written alongside the symbol or inside the packaging.

Legislation

Legislation protects the user or consumer and must be complied with when making products or employing people. If a company or an individual is shown to have broken the law, they can be **prosecuted**.

- The Health and Safety at Work Act 1974 (HASAWA) covers a wide range of duties for both employers and employees in the workplace.

- Children's toys are covered by specific toy safety legislation.

- Further legislation exists for products depending on their particular nature. These include: electrical products, gas powered products, products that work under high pressure, products that involve pyrotechnics, explosives, or emit loud noises or electromagnetic fields.

Figure 1.45: Employers are required to provide personal protective equipment (PPE) if there is a risk to a worker's heath and safety

Legislation relating to a product would be very important to consider when designing any product as it is enforced by law and could prevent a product being manufactured or result in legal action.

Planned obsolescence

The machinery used to manufacture cars used to need replacing every three years. Car manufacturers saw this as a good opportunity to change and update their design at the same time. By releasing a new model and stopping production of parts for the old one, it becomes out of date or obsolete. This is an example of **planned obsolescence**.

There are four main types of planned obsolescence still commonly used today. The main objective of companies using these is to make customers buy new replacement products from them. Contrived durability and prevention of repair are particularly important as they are factored in by the engineer at the design stage.

- **Contrived durability** This is where a product is designed to be unreliable and stop working after a length of time.

- **Prevention of repair** Companies may choose to market products that are intentionally difficult to take apart or repair. Some children's toys have batteries fixed inside them so they cannot be replaced.

- **Software compatibility** As technology gets better, the programs and files it uses and relies upon become more complex, larger or have different requirements. As such, any product an engineer designs is likely to eventually become out of date. An engineer may be tasked with designing a product that is simply more compatible than its predecessor.

- **Perceived obsolescence** On the surface this has less to do with product manufacture and more to do with marketing. Companies highlight the advantages of new or alternative products to try to convince customers their older product is no longer suitable. An engineer may be tasked with designing a new product to address the flaws or weaknesses of a previous iteration.

Sustainable design (6Rs)

Sustainable design means reducing the impact of a product so it can be produced, used and disposed of with minimal effect on the environment. Making a product sustainable means it can continue to be made without running out of materials or causing significant environmental damage. Sustainable products are also viewed more favourably by customers.

The 6Rs are a range of considerations that you can use to influence your design to make it more sustainable.

Table 1.17: The 6Rs and their definitions

6Rs	Definition
Reduce	Cut down the amount of material used as much as possible.
Recycle	Reprocess a material or product to make something else.
Reuse	Use a product to make something else with all or parts of it.
Refuse	Do not use excessive packaging or materials that are bad for the environment.
Rethink	Design in a way that considers people and the environment.
Repair	When a product breaks down or stops working properly, fix it.

Reduce

Reducing means designing something to use the minimum amount of materials and processes required. This minimises the impact the product has on the environment.

Companies that package Easter eggs are often criticised for the amount of empty space that is included in the design. If you compare the wasted space in a regular egg box with an Easter egg box, there is a significant difference. While this space might make the product look bigger and better value from outside and may help sales, it uses more materials than is necessary.

Figure 1.46: Easter eggs are often sold in plastic and cardboard containers for decoration

Recycle

Recycling is turning the materials from one unwanted product into something else. Products are separated into different material types and those materials are reshaped into a completely new product. This prevents the materials going into landfill.

Some materials recycle better than others. Materials such as plastic degrade and produce a poorer product when recycled, but this doesn't make them unusable. A good example is RPB material which is made from shredding plastic water bottles and making them into fleece for jumpers.

Figure 1.47: Single use plastic bottles form the majority of our recycling waste

Materials such as metal or glass produce a product of very similar quality and this allows them to be recycled over and over. Apple chose glass and aluminium for their phone casings to improve the environmental impact of their products.

The disadvantage of recycling is that the reprocessing of the material still requires energy and often produces pollution to achieve.

Reuse

Reusing is creating a new purpose for a product, or parts of a product, once it has finished being useful. Often these solutions are hand-made and involve creativity on the part of the customer – such as turning old water bottles into planters. Creating a second purpose for a product that is efficient and that a customer would be happy with is a complicated design task.

Figure 1.48: A planter made from a plastic bottle

Refuse

Refusing means to do without something altogether. Some parts of a product may be unnecessary for function. They might have been added for aesthetic value. Ask yourself: would removing the unnecessary parts be possible? Online delivery companies have been criticised for this – products are often posted inside one or more larger boxes with additional packaging.

Figure 1.49: Excessive delivery packaging

Rethink

Rethinking means completely changing strategy on a product. This is often done on existing products that are poor for the environment. Engineers will consider the product and look at completely different solutions to do the same job with less environmental damage. Rethinking might mean changing the design of a product, changing materials, changing processes or creating a completely different design that achieves the same function. Compostable waste bags are a great example of rethinking, solving the same problem from a different approach and eliminating the amount of non-degradable plastic being put into the ground.

Figure 1.50: Compostable bag for food waste

Repair

Repairing a product extends its usable life, so prevents the need to buy a new, replacement product. As an engineer you can consider making sure the inside of your product is accessible. You can design parts to be removable and replaceable.

Many countries, including the UK, have introduced a 'right to repair' law, requiring products to be repairable and have replacement parts manufactured for them.

Figure 1.51: Repairing a bicycle

Over to you! 3

Consider a child's bicycle.

1   How has the designer of the bicycle tried to make it easier to repair?

2   There will eventually be a time when the child is too big for the bike. List all the possible things that may happen to it then. Which are best for the environment?

3   If the bike is broken beyond repair, how does its design allow it to be recycled?

Test your knowledge 3

1   What happens when a product is recycled?

2   How does designing for repair reduce the environmental impact of a product?

3   Evaluate how sustainable card drinks cups from fast food restaurants are.

Design for the circular economy

Many products used to be produced with no concern for where the materials came from, used, and then buried in landfill. This wasteful approach is called a linear economy. It is harmful to the environment and cannot be sustained forever as pollution builds up and materials run out. Sustainability has become an important topic and companies and customers increasingly have an interest in environmental issues.

Modern design thinking aims to create products that are more sympathetic to the environment. Designers, companies and customers all have a part to play in ensuring as much material as possible is reused and a minimum amount of materials are disposed of as landfill. This model is called the **circular economy** and is summarised by the cycle in Figure 1.52. A product goes through this cycle until it cannot be used again and is disposed of. As an engineer, you can design products that are better for the environment by considering how they are treated at different stages of their life cycle.

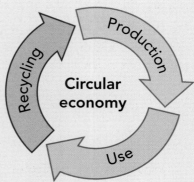

Figure 1.52: The three main steps in a circular economy

Raw materials

The choice of raw material is very important. Some materials are finite. This means they will eventually run out and cannot be replaced. The fossil fuels that are used in the production of plastic, for example, took millions of years to form and are being used up much faster than they are produced.

Some materials can be grown and so are considered sustainable. Fast growing plants like bamboo can be planted and used to make products. By growing more bamboo, there will always be a supply. Wood from forests that are controlled can similarly be maintained. In many locations around the globe, deforestation takes place without replacing the trees, causing climate problems.

Figure 1.53: Plates and cutlery made from bamboo are more sustainable than those made from plastic

Production

Designers can consider the environmental impact of the processes needed for their product. Some processes are more harmful than others. As a designer you could consider the possible ways to manufacture the parts of the product and choose those that are least wasteful and produce least pollution. This may not always be the most popular choice with the client as it is not necessarily the cheapest. Even using recycled material or recycling a material has a cost and sometimes that cost is higher than the raw material in the first place.

Factories also typically require a lot of energy. Partly because of this demand and the processes they undertake, factories produce the majority of pollution on the planet. They can consider ways to reduce their impact, using green sources of energy such as solar, tidal, geothermal or wind. This type of energy is naturally replenished and is called renewable energy.

Figure 1.54: A chemical factory and solar plant

Transportation

To manufacture a product, materials must be sourced and moved to a suitable manufacturing facility. Often this requires transporting goods between countries. Transportation requires fuel and causes pollution. As with manufacturing, transportation has a carbon footprint.

The best way to prevent this is to keep the whole process as localised as possible. If you could find a suitable material nearby and manufacture it close to that site, you would minimise your transportation impacts.

Case study

Bioplastics

Plastic waste is a well-documented problem. Disposable plastics are dumped in landfill and make their way into the sea. Estimates suggest there are more than eight billion tonnes of plastic products in the world right now and six billion of that is waste. Plastic waste also takes up to 1000 years to degrade so is a serious long-term problem.

One modern solution is to manufacture bioplastics. These materials mimic the look and feel of plastic but are made from plant materials such as starch and corn oil. This means the product doesn't rely on fossil fuels to be made.

Using a natural material also presents new opportunities when it reaches the end of its life. These products can be composted or if they do end up in landfill can break down in just a few months. Typically, however, they can't be recycled into new plastic products like conventional plastics.

Figure 1.55: Bioplastics are made from renewable resources

A concern is the land and farming required to provide for our huge plastic demand. Farming produces pollution and requires chemicals that end up in the environment. The area of farmland that would be required to provide for our huge plastic demand would also be incredibly large, limiting living space and farmland producing food crops.

Check your understanding

1   Identify which of the 6Rs is addressed by changing to bioplastics.

2   Explain why using bioplastic might be most effective on products with short lives such as water bottles.

3   Evaluate whether using bioplastics would contribute positively to the circular economy.

Stretch

Engineers have to consider a wide range of influences when designing to create a successful outcome. Some influences include:

- material availability

- sustainability

- legislation.

Choose one of the design influences. With examples, describe how that design influence makes a difference to the design you are producing and the choices you have to make as a designer.

Review your learning

Test your knowledge   4

1   What does ACCESS FM stand for?

2   What are the differences between one-off and mass production?

3   Explain what the 6Rs are and how they influence design.

4   Explain how legislation influences the design of a product.

What have you learnt?

	See section
• What types of criteria are included in a design specification.	2.1
• How manufacturing considerations affect design.	2.2
• What influences affect engineering product design.	2.3

Communicating design outcomes

Let's get started

Designers visualising ideas use many different drawing techniques, from fast, inaccurate methods through to incredibly detailed and time-consuming diagrams.

If you're a creative person you probably have many ideas running through your head every day. How do you record those ideas or act on them? What should you make a note of for later? How much time should go into recording it?

What will you learn?

*   The types of drawing used in engineering.
*   Types of working drawing.
*   Using computer aided design (CAD) software and its benefits.

3.1 Types of drawing used in engineering

Freehand sketching

The best method for generating and recording designs is **freehand sketching**. When designers are thinking about new products, they will create quick ideas using freehand sketches. Having this visual record allows you to compare ideas and show others the ideas, in case you need an external opinion.

Freehand drawing can be **2D** or **3D**, but is typically done without any technical drawing equipment. You don't need rulers, set squares, compasses or stencils. At this stage it is OK if the drawings are not technically accurate – you are just trying to create a 'feel'

Figure 1.56: Sketching without any specialist equipment

for the ideas. Don't worry if you are not the most confident at drawing. It is not about creating an artistic masterpiece. Your goal is just to convey information about your idea.

It doesn't have to be just drawings – adding notes and annotations can help explain parts of your designs that can't be easily seen or conveyed through drawing. Details such as a battery compartment or details on the back of a design, for example, might be better explained with a short label or note.

Oblique

Oblique drawing is probably the quickest and simplest 3D drawing method you can work with. It allows you to sketch an idea quickly and easily. It requires more control than freehand drawing and requires simple drawing tools such as a ruler and set square to construct well.

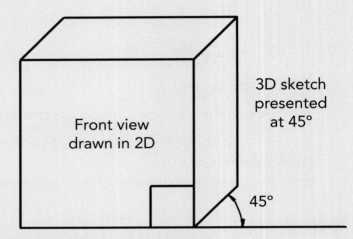

You may have seen or tried oblique drawing before. Usually, the front of your product (the most detailed side) is drawn in 2D then lines are drawn out at 45 degrees to represent depth. There are two main types of oblique drawing: cavalier oblique and cabinet oblique.

Figure 1.57: Oblique drawing

Cavalier oblique

In **cavalier oblique** you draw out all lines at the correct size using the actual measurements. This means you can take measurements off the drawing to check the proportions, so it is really good for conveying size information. The problem is it distorts the image, stretching it into the page.

Use a ruler to measure the shape in Figure 1.58. All of the sides measure the same. It measures as a cube, but it looks like a rectangle. As well as not being able to see how it might appear in real life, this may cause confusion with anyone you share the design with.

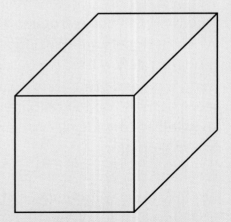

Figure 1.58: A cube drawn in cavalier oblique

Cabinet oblique

In **cabinet oblique** the lines showing the depth of the design are made shorter. In Figure 1.59, the depth lines (the receding axis) have been made half the length they should be. This means the design starts to look more like the cube we intended to draw.

However, if you take a ruler you will see that taking measurements from this drawing is not possible. It no longer measures as a cube. Because it allows you to quickly make decisions about the look of the product, most designers choose to draw in cabinet rather than cavalier oblique – concerning themselves with measured technical drawings later on.

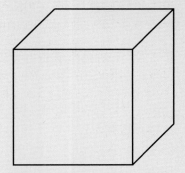

Figure 1.59: A cube drawn in cabinet oblique

Test your knowledge **1**

1   What angle is used in oblique drawings to create a 3D effect?
2   What are the advantages of oblique drawing instead of 2D?
3   Explain why oblique drawings are not necessarily suitable for taking dimensions from.

Isometric

Isometric drawing gives a more realistic-looking 3D drawing than oblique but can be tricky to draw at first. Isometric drawing is used all over the world in lots of engineering areas, so it is well understood.

Figure 1.60: Isometric projection creates a more realistic image

Figure 1.61: Isometric drawing is often used in computer games for clarity and accuracy

Isometric drawing follows two simple rules:

1   All vertical lines (the height of your design) remain vertical.

2   All horizontal lines (the width and the depth) are drawn at 30 degrees.

None of the lines require shortening. This means the isometric design both looks right and can be used for measurements – something that couldn't be done in oblique.

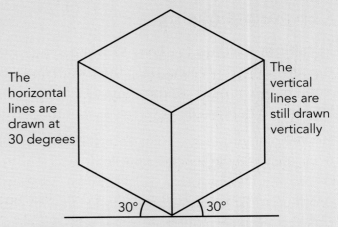

Figure 1.62: Rules for creating isometric projections

Orthographic drawings

Orthographic drawings are working drawings that present three different 2D views of your product to show what it is like. The design is drawn from the front, side and plan (top) views. These designs are often used by manufacturers to help plan production.

As they are used when manufacturing the design, orthographic drawings have to be very accurate. They must have a scale and show dimensions and all three views must use the same scale. Because of this importance, they have their own guidelines and rules to make sure they are drawn in a specific way; these are covered in greater detail in Section 3.2, Working drawings.

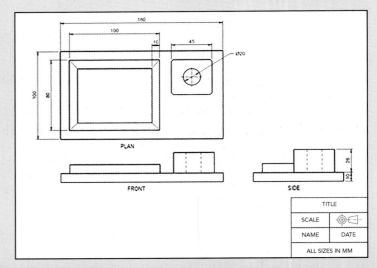

Figure 1.63: Orthographic drawing of a desk tidy

Exploded views

Exploded views are used to show how the parts of an object fit together. As you can see in Figure 1.64, they are neat, easy to read and informative about the assembly of the product.

Assembly drawings

Assembly drawings are drawn in isometric and usually exploded to help explain how parts fit together. Assembly drawings will always refer to the complete product and parts.

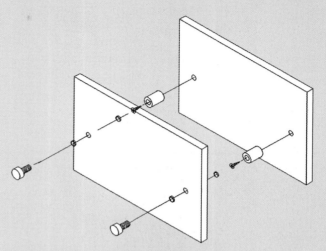

Figure 1.64: Exploded isometric drawing

As well as an exploded diagram, assembly drawings contain notes and instructions required to complete the product. Examples of details used in the drawing might include:

- a parts list including names or reference numbers of parts if using bought in components

- quantities of parts required

- instructional notes to help with assembly

- references to other technical drawings

- specification requirements of specific parts

- any other details of use specific to the design.

They are a type of isometric drawing so follow all of the drawing rules for isometric but also have another couple of rules of their own:

- The parts are arranged so that each can be clearly seen and identified.

- The positions in relation to each other are maintained – so screws for example still line up with the holes they fit into.

Creating an exploded view is a bit like taking apart a product and carefully laying out the pieces so you can see how they fit together. Note that it doesn't contain details on material choice or any processes needed to fit the parts together. These would have to be provided separately and would make this drawing into an assembly drawing.

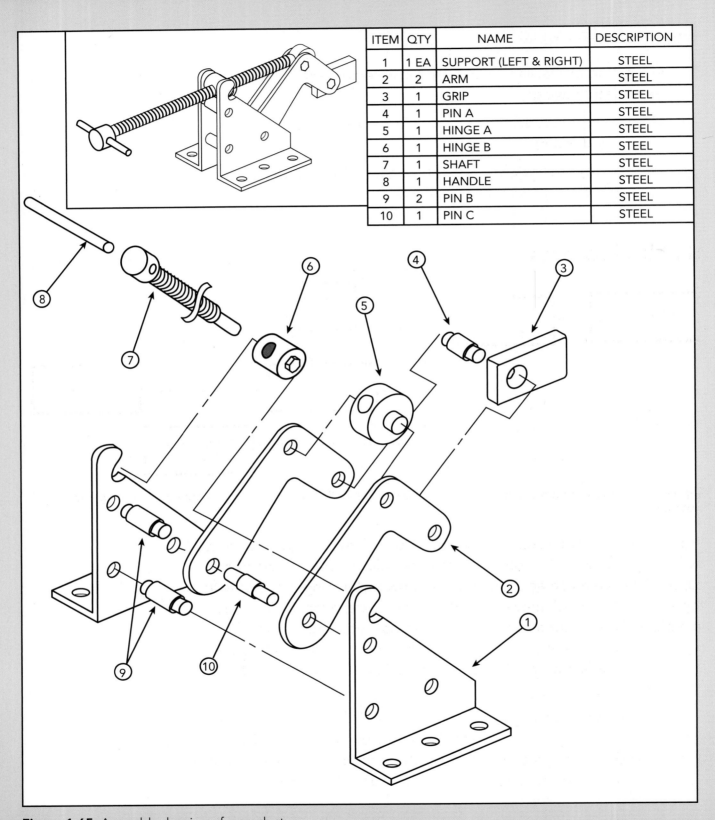

ITEM	QTY	NAME	DESCRIPTION
1	1 EA	SUPPORT (LEFT & RIGHT)	STEEL
2	2	ARM	STEEL
3	1	GRIP	STEEL
4	1	PIN A	STEEL
5	1	HINGE A	STEEL
6	1	HINGE B	STEEL
7	1	SHAFT	STEEL
8	1	HANDLE	STEEL
9	2	PIN B	STEEL
10	1	PIN C	STEEL

Figure 1.65: Assembly drawing of a product

Test your knowledge   3

1   What type of drawing style is used in assembly and exploded drawings?

2   Describe the purpose of the centre line in exploded and assembly drawings.

3   Explain why flat pack furniture retailers will often include an assembly diagram with their products.

Block diagrams

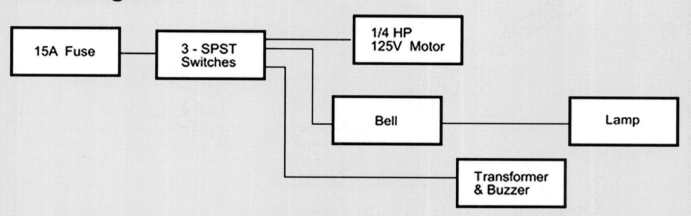

Figure 1.66: Block diagram of a fume extractor blower. The bell and lamp turn on to provide a warning if the system fails.

Block diagrams are a system in which parts or functions are represented by blocks connected by lines that show the relationships between the blocks. They aren't an actual diagram of how these things physically fit together or are wired, they just explain which parts affect each other. In a block diagram for a hand drill, for instance, you might have blocks representing the battery, the trigger and the motor all linked together because they affect each other when the drill is operated.

Block diagrams are used for the design and analysis of a system. They are really useful when planning out electrical wiring for instance because you can see which component parts have to influence each other. They can also be used by a designer with limited electrical knowledge as they don't describe how the components are wired but just how they interact with each other.

Flowcharts

Flowcharts are a type of diagram that represent a workflow or a process. They show a step-by-step approach to solving a task. They use various kinds of boxes and their order is shown by connecting the boxes with arrows.

Table 1.18: Symbols used in flowcharts and their meaning

Symbol	Name	Function
	Start/End	An oval represents the start or the end point of the process
	Arrow	An arrow show which processes are connected and in which direction you should follow the chart
	Process	A rectangular process block represents something happening
	Input	An input block represents an input being made or a situation changing
	Decision	A decision block has different outcomes to follow depending on a condition. Decisions can be made with 'yes' and 'no' loops, which are arrows going to different parts of the process depending on whether the answer is 'yes' or 'no'

You might use a flowchart when designing to explain how a product works. You could explain what happens when you switch your product on or what happens when the product senses certain conditions.

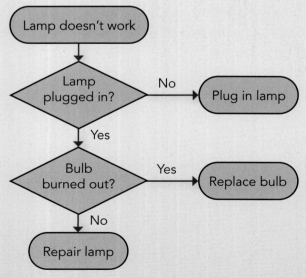

Figure 1.67: A simple flowchart to troubleshoot a broken lamp

Circuit and wiring diagrams

Circuit diagrams are conventional graphical representations of an electrical circuit. They are used for the design, construction and maintenance of electrical and electronic equipment. Circuit diagrams use symbols representing different components, which you may have seen in science or electronics lessons.

Wiring diagrams are simplified pictorial representations of a circuit and show how the components should be connected.

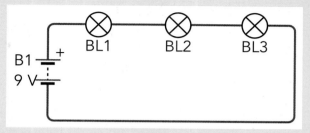

Figure 1.68: A circuit diagram showing three light bulbs and a 9 V battery connected in series (one after the other)

This means they look more like pictures of the actual parts you are fitting together, which gives you a good idea where the connection points are on the components and an idea of what tools and connectors are needed.

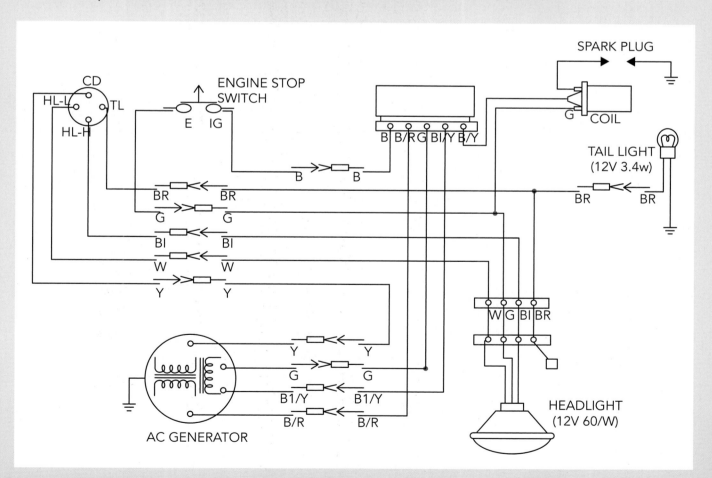

Figure 1.69: Wiring diagram for a headlight in a car

Over to you!

1   Research flowcharts and find some examples of flowcharts for various processes.

2   Produce a simple flowchart for your morning routine using process blocks: getting up, having breakfast and going out.

3   Use decision blocks and process blocks to make a flowchart for making a piece of toast. You may need to decide if it is cooked enough and what toppings you want on it.

3.2 Working drawings

2D engineering drawings using third angle orthographic projection

Working drawings, like the one shown in Figure 1.70, provide technical information to a manufacturer so they know how to make the product. They contain a range of symbols, line types and notes.

Front, plan and side views

Frame with grid reference system

Dimensions

Title block containing name, title, date, scale and third angle orthographic projection symbol

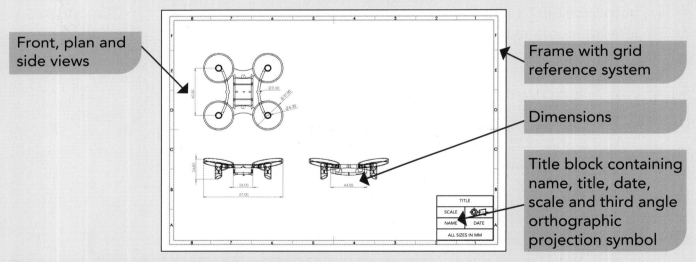

Figure 1.70: Orthographic drawing of a drone

A **third angle orthographic projection** is a type of working drawing.
As seen in Figure 1.71, it shows three different 2D views of a part
(front, plan and side).

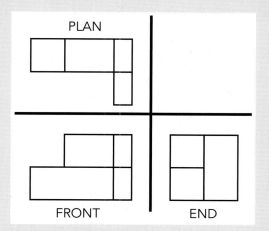

Figure 1.71: A third angle projection layout

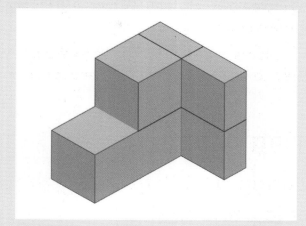

Figure 1.72: 3D image of the shape depicted in Figure 1.71

The symbol for third angle orthographic projection is shown in Figure 1.73.
The shapes represent the top and side views of a cone. This symbol
should be included in the title block of third angle orthographic projection
drawings (as demonstrated in Figures 1.74 and 1.75).

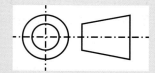

Figure 1.73: The third
angle orthographic
projection symbol

Standard conventions

If designers all worked in completely different ways, other designers and
manufacturers might have difficulty interpreting their drawings. Misreading
a technical drawing could cause errors costing time and money.

To prevent these mistakes, engineers have agreed ways of drawing
and a set of rules on how to lay those drawings out. These **standard
conventions** are agreed rules that set the drawing standards used in
engineering. The following conventions should be used when creating
an orthographic drawing.

Title block

An orthographic drawing has a 10mm border around the edge.
The drawing also needs to include a **title block**. This will contain the title
of the drawing and other key details about the drawing.

A title block can be a strip along the bottom of the diagram, as in Figure 1.74. Note that the text is in the middle of the bar, and the gap above the text is the same as the gap below the text.

The title block should contain the author's name, the scale, the drawing title, the units used and the date it was created. It may also be presented as a box in the bottom right corner, as in Figure 1.75. As before, the text should be in the middle of each row, with the gap above the text the same as the gap below.

| NAME | | SCALE | TITLE | ALL SIZES IN MM | DATE |

Figure 1.74: Title block as a bar along the bottom of the page

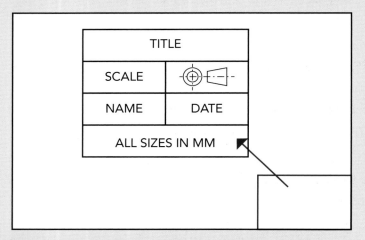

Figure 1.75: Title block in the right-hand corner

Metric units of measurement

On technical drawings in the UK, measurements are added using the metric system. Usually, this means using millimetres on your drawings. It is very useful to have a good idea how millimetres, centimetres and metres compare to each other. Designing a building 100 mm tall instead of 10 000 mm tall would be a real problem.

0.1 cm = 1 mm	1 cm = 10 mm
0.001 m = 1 mm	1 m = 1000 mm

On the title block of the diagram you should be able to see a note reading 'all measurements/dimensions in mm' that confirms this. Obviously, if you are designing a product it is really important that the manufacturer knows exactly which unit of measurement has been used, otherwise the final product could be a completely different size.

Scale

Toy cars are made much smaller than the real thing but still keep the same proportions. Toys like the one in Figure 1.76 are often produced at 1:64 **scale** or smaller. This means the toy is 64 times smaller than the real thing. 1 cm on this toy car would represent 64 cm on the real car.

In a similar way you can't always draw your design full size. For example, full-size drawings of cars or buildings would be gigantic. Because of this, designers use scale to keep their drawings accurate but a manageable size. This involves making the drawing bigger or smaller by a fixed amount.

Figure 1.76: Toy car models are often a scale model of the real thing

A scale of 1:1 means the drawing is full size. You can take measurements directly from the drawing.

A scale of 1:2 would mean the drawing is half the actual size. This is useful for drawing larger objects, but any measurement taken directly from the drawing would have to be doubled.

A scale of 2:1 would mean the drawing is twice the actual size. This is useful for drawing very small objects, but any measurement taken directly from the drawing would have to be halved.

Table 1.19: Some typical scales

Object	Scale	What it means
A building	1:200	Each 1 cm on the design would mean 200 cm in real life
A car	1:20	Each 1 cm on the design would mean 20 cm in real life
A microchip	5:1	Each 5 cm on the drawing would mean 1 cm in real life

If an orthographic drawing has 'not to scale' written in its title block, it means it has not been drawn to accurate proportions. This means you cannot take any measurements off it and, though it still might give you an idea of what the product looks like and may have some sizes written on it, it is no use for presenting information about dimensions.

Test your knowledge   4

1   If a drawing has scale 1:5 and a component measures 100mm on the drawing, how big is it in real life?

2   If a product measures 1500mm in length and you want to draw it to a scale of 1:20, how long would the drawing be?

3   Explain why scale 200:1 is not a suitable scale to draw a building.

Tolerance

Manufacturing is not always an exact process. Often, products are made marginally smaller, larger or with imperfections. If you went into a workshop and drilled 100 holes, they wouldn't all perfectly line up with each other. Errors can also happen through human error and wear and tear on the machinery.

Tolerance is the way you as an engineer can tell the manufacturer how much error is acceptable before the product is considered unacceptable and/or faulty. This means it's really useful when considering quality.

Tight tolerance

Tight tolerance means high precision. The component needs to be very accurate. (Remember, if you have very little tolerance, you are easily offended!) Telescopes and scientific equipment have tight tolerance. The parts must be manufactured very precisely so the product is reliable and trustworthy.

Loose tolerance

Loose tolerance means low precision. The size of the component can be relatively inaccurate and still be acceptable. (Remember, if you are very tolerant, you are very accepting and easy going.) An example of a low precision product is a pair of slippers; if they are not absolutely accurate it is not too much of a problem.

High precision products are expensive to make. The machines and processes used must be extremely accurate and parts will need to be maintained or replaced more often to ensure consistent accuracy. There will inevitably be more wasted products that don't fit within tolerance as well. For these reasons, products that don't require tight tolerance, such as children's toys or cartons, are made to a larger tolerance.

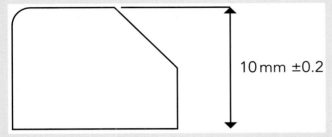

10 mm ±0.2

Figure 1.77: A dimension arrow with tolerance stated

To explain tolerance, you add a ± symbol after the dimension and then state how much the dimension can be out by. Figure 1.77 shows a dimension of 10 mm with a tolerance of 0.2 mm. The 0.2 mm can be thought of as goalposts – anything 0.2 mm either side of 10 mm is a goal. Anything more than 0.2 mm outside this is a miss and unacceptable. In the example shown, the design can be any size between 9.8 mm and 10.2 mm and still be considered acceptable.

Test your knowledge   5

1   Why might electronic components be manufactured to tight tolerance?

2   Describe why all products are not manufactured to high precision.

3   A plastic component is described as being 140 mm ±0.8. Calculate the smallest and largest acceptable size the part could be to remain in tolerance.

Standard conventions for dimensions

Linear measurements

In orthographic drawings, there are very particular rules about the way you add your size **dimensions**. These rules are agreed and recorded and used by engineers and designers everywhere. Using these rules means that engineers and manufacturers can clearly read each other's designs so there are no miscommunications.

- Dimension and projection lines are thinner than the drawing lines. The projection line comes within 1 mm of your drawing but doesn't actually touch it.

- Dimension lines should touch the projection line with a small filled-in arrowhead at each end.

- The shortest dimensions are placed closest to the drawing. Longer dimensions are positioned further away.

- **Linear measurements**, usually in **mm**, are written in the middle of each dimension line. The measurements are written above the dimension lines such that they can be read from the bottom or the right only.

- Whenever possible dimension lines should be outside the shape.

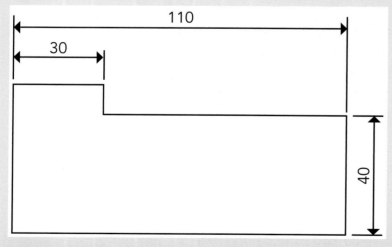

Figure 1.78: Linear dimension lines added to a simple shape

Radius and diameter

Showing the size of a curve or circle is slightly different, as you might imagine. Measurements of a circle or an arc are prefixed with either **R** to show the **radius** or Ø for **diameter**, as in Figure 1.79.

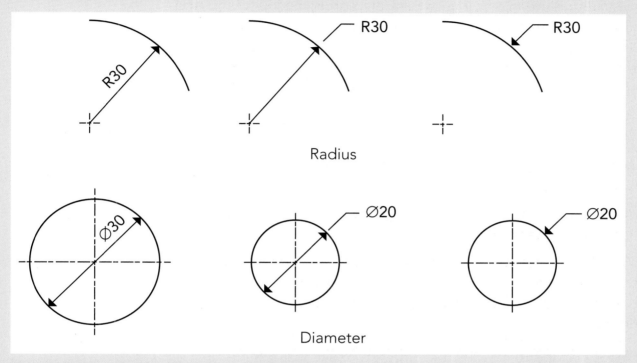

Figure 1.79: Dimensions added to arcs and circles

The dimension can be put inside the shape along the radius or diameter (unlike the dimensioning for a straight line, which needs to be outside the shape). Often there isn't enough space to clearly put the dimensions inside the circle or curve so an extended line pointing to the curve is used on the outside of the shape.

Test your knowledge   6

1   State what units are normally used for dimensions in third angle drawing.

2   Explain how you make sure projection lines and dimension lines don't look like part of the drawing.

3   Explain when you would use the Ø symbol on a diagram.

Surface finish

Many products are manufactured with an acceptable finish. Plastics, for instance, usually have a reasonably smooth finish on them when they are processed and often don't need any further work. Some materials and products require a finish to be applied to make that surface smooth enough. To indicate this a surface finish symbol is added. Designers use the **surface finish** symbol to advise manufacturing engineers on the **machined finish** a product should have.

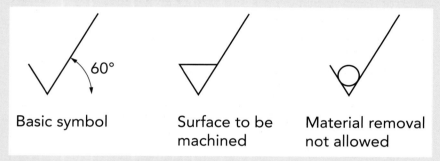

Basic symbol   Surface to be machined   Material removal not allowed

Figure 1.80: Three types of surface finish symbol

The symbol is added on the surface that needs to be smooth. It looks like a tick shape with both sides at 60 degrees to the material. The basic symbol is used if the material is to be smoothed, for example by sanding. If a machine is needed to remove the surface to make it smooth a horizontal line is added across the tick to make a triangle shape. A circle is added in the tick if no material removal is to be used on the surface, but it still needs to be a certain finish.

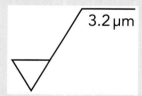

Figure 1.81: Surface finish symbol with accuracy stated

To say how accurate the surface needs to be, you can add a roughness value to the top of the tick. The number is measured in micrometres, so in the example in Figure 1.81, 3.2 µm means any imperfections must be 0.0032 mm or smaller.

Meaning of line types

Different types of line have different meaning in orthographic drawing. While this makes your drawing more complicated to draw it also prevents any confusion as to what each line means and allows you to communicate more information.

Table 1.20: Orthographic drawing line conventions

Line type	Description	Appearance
Outlines	presented thicker than other lines on the drawing	————————
Hidden detail	thick lines drawn as a dashed line	- - - - - - - - -
Centre line	dot and dash sequence	— · — · — · —
Projection	continuous thin lines	————————
Leader line	connects a graphical representation on the drawing to some text	
Dimension	medium line with solid arrowheads on each end	◄————————►

Outlines

Outlines are the lines used to draw the shape of your product. They are presented thicker than other lines on the drawing. Obviously this is slightly easier to do on a computer compared to hand drawing, but can be achieved by using a darker pencil (for example, an HB for outlines and a 2H for all other lines) or using fineliners of different nib thicknesses. This means when someone reads your drawing, outlines won't be confused with dimension arrows and projection lines.

Because they describe the shape of your product, outlines are the most important lines. If there is a situation where one line type needs to be drawn over the top of another, the outline is the one that is drawn.

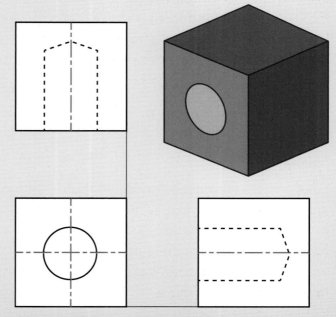

Figure 1.82: Orthographic drawing demonstrating outlines, hidden detail and centre lines

Hidden detail

Hidden detail lines are also thick lines but are drawn as a dashed line. They show where parts of your product are hidden by the part of the product you are looking at. There is no rule as to how long the dashes and gaps have to be but you should try to keep the same lengths and spacings for all hidden detail lines on the same page.

Centre line

Centre lines use a dot and dash sequence. They use a thin line rather than a thick one. Centre lines, as the name suggests, show where the centre of a component is, for example, the centre of a screw hole.

Centre lines enable a manufacturer to measure where the centre of a drill or other cutting machine needs to be, so the holes they make will be in the correct places.

Projection

Projection lines are continuous thin lines. They are used to extend your drawing and make sure the next angle you view lines up with the first one. They should start 1 mm away from your drawing and extend up or across so the next view lines up.

Dimension

A medium line with solid arrowheads on each end is used to show the distances on the drawing.

Leader lines

Leader lines connect a graphical representation on the drawing to some text. It's a bit like adding a label to your diagram where you might need to explain a detail. Different types of leader line may be used for different parts.

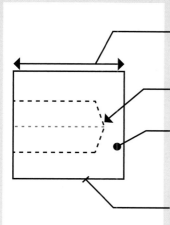

A **dimension leader line** has no end on it, but connects to a dimension line. It is used when you want to add a note about the size.

A **closed arrow leader** line has a solid arrow on it, similar to a dimension line. It points to a feature than needs further explanation.

A **dot ended leader line** has a filled circle on the end of it. It is used where you want to give information about the face of a design.

A **tick leader line** ends in a short, broad dash. It is used when you want to give information about an edge.

Figure 1.83: Four types of leader line

Test your knowledge   7

1   How do you differentiate your drawing outlines from the other lines on the diagram?

2   Explain where you might use a centre line and what its purpose is.

3   What is the purpose of a leader line and when might you need one?

Abbreviations

Designers use standard **abbreviations** to communicate their drawing requirements to the manufacturers. Having a standard list of abbreviations means other engineers and manufacturers know what you mean, regardless of what language they speak. Abbreviations also save space on the drawings, which often get quite busy with lines and information.

The full list of abbreviations is in the British Standard BS 8888. Table 1.21 shows some of the more common ones.

Table 1.21: Some common standard abbreviations used in design

Term	Abbreviation
Across flats	AF
Centre line	CL
Diameter (in a note)	DIA
Diameter (preceding a dimension)	Ø
Drawing	DRG
Material	MAT
Square (in a note)	SQ
Square (preceding a dimension)	▢

Across flats

In some cases it is possible to take measurements on different parts of a design. Imagine drawing the hexagon-shaped head of a bolt. Measuring from corner to corner gives a longer measurement than measuring from side to side. A measurement between flat sides is called 'across flats'.

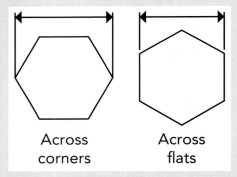

Across corners   Across flats

Figure 1.84: Dimensions made corner to corner and across the flat sides

Where a dimension is taken across the flat sides, the abbreviation **AF** can be added to avoid any confusion.

Centre line

When you draw a centre line marking the centre of a component or hole, you use a dashed line. When you refer to the centre line in notes you can use the abbreviation **CL**.

Diameter

When you draw a circle, for example a drilled hole, you use the symbol Ø on the diagram. When you refer to the diameter in notes you can use the abbreviation **DIA**.

Drawing

Referring to the drawing in notes, you can use the abbreviation **DRG**.

Material

On the drawing, different materials are indicated by using different cross hatching and textures. In notes, materials are referred to with the abbreviation **MAT**.

Square

The dimension **SQ** is often added to the drawing or notes where a shape is square. This is similar to the way a diameter or radius symbol is used for a circle.

Representations of mechanical features

Designers use a wide range of symbols to advise the manufacturer about the **mechanical features** required on a product. These are some common features and what they look like when drawn.

Holes

A hole is a connection point for screws, bolts or other components to fit into. They are quite easy to represent using the line types you have already looked at. From the front, a hole appears as a solid, circular outline drawn on the shape. From the side, a hole is drawn using hidden detail lines showing where each edge of the hole is.

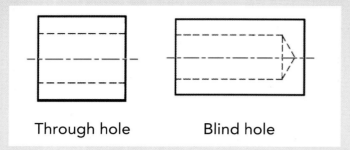

Figure 1.85: A blind hole is made to a specified depth; a through hole goes completely through the material

This gives the manufacturer enough information to be able to measure the diameter of the hole and the depth of the hole. The centre line allows them to measure where they need to line up a drill or other machine to create the hole.

Threads and chamfers

Accurately drawing the thread that goes around the outside of a screw would be time-consuming and unnecessarily complicated. Fortunately, there is an orthographic drawing convention for threaded components.

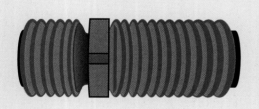
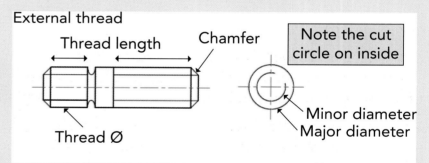

Figure 1.86: A component with an external thread and its representation in orthographic drawing

An external thread is a thread cut into the outside of the part, as on a screw or the component in Figure 1.86. You show the depth of the thread using two parallel lines on the side view. One set of lines represents the widest part of the thread and a second set represents the narrowest. On the front view, where you can see the diameter of the thread, you show this by drawing an incomplete circle for the narrowest diameter and a complete circle for the widest.

Of course, some diameter or radius dimensions would also be very helpful here to assist with manufacturing.

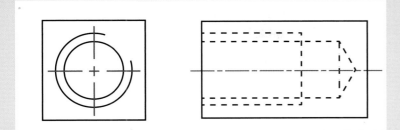

Figure 1.87: An internal thread represented in orthographic drawing

An internal thread is cut into the inside of the part so you can screw something into it. You show the depth of the thread using two parallel hidden lines on the side view, as shown in Figure 1.87. On the front view, where you can see the diameter of the thread, you show this by drawing an incomplete circle for the outside diameter.

This is quite a complex detail so it is perfectly acceptable to add a leader line and some notation explaining the detail.

A chamfer is a sloping edge cut into the corner of two sides. Chamfers are incorporated to remove sharp edges, which prevents damage to other parts of the product and protects the user from injury.

Countersinks

A countersink is a well that a screw head sits in, so it doesn't stick out of the material. The countersink is made by adding the well around the top of the hole, as in Figure 1.88, before the product is assembled.

As quite a common feature, you may frequently need to add countersinks to your technical drawings. You will also need to mark an angle at the top of the countersink. This is the angle from one edge of the hole to the other.

Figure 1.88: A countersink hole prepared to receive the screw head

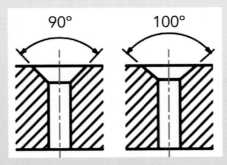

Figure 1.89: Countersinks represented in orthographic drawing

As with dimension lines, there should be projection lines nearly touching the edge of the drawing. The dimension line itself should be curved in an arc and the measurement should be the angle of the head in degrees. There will probably be some other dimensions added too.

> **Hands on!**
>
> 1   Draw an orthographic drawing of a bolt with a thread along its length. You can use any dimensions you choose.
>
> 2   Add a chamfer to the end of the bolt.
>
> 3   Draw a block with a hole cut into it and an internal thread that will match your bolt.

Knurls

Knurling is putting ridges in a pattern on a material. It adds grip so the user can turn or lift a part more easily. On the pocket watch in Figure 1.90, a straight knurl pattern has been added around the controls so they can be easily turned and the user's fingers don't slip on them. You might want to add knurling to handle grips or controls.

To represent knurling on your technical drawings, you add a pattern to the part that has the texture. Note that the knurl doesn't fill the entire area and is drawn using much thinner lines than the outlines.

Figure 1.90: Straight knurling adding grip to the controls

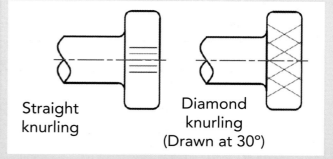

Straight knurling

Diamond knurling (Drawn at 30°)

Figure 1.91: Knurling represented in orthographic drawing

3.3 Using CAD drawing software

The drawing techniques in this section can also be created using CAD software. In modern engineering, using CAD is one of the most popular ways to create and present 2D and 3D design ideas.

CAD programs are often paid for software and specialise in 2D vector drawings or 3D modelling software. Some CAD software allows you to transition a design between the two, creating a flat orthographic projection from a 3D model, for example.

Using CAD drawing software compared to manual drawing techniques

The advantages to any software also apply to CAD drawing: images are easily edited, simple mistakes can easily be undone, and a change in the design can be easily incorporated. Obviously, adjusting a technically accurate orthographic drawn by hand is much more complicated and can involve starting from scratch.

Figure 1.92: An engineer using CAD software to design part of a medical syringe

Once familiar with a program, images and drawings are quick to produce. Common shapes or parts can be saved and reused or built upon. Engineers working in 3D will have a library of previously-created shapes and images to draw upon.

Communicating design proposals to a client is a key consideration. CAD drawings are easily sent to a client, manufacturer or other engineer. This is useful where regular feedback or input from specialists is required.

Table 1.22: Advantages and limitations of CAD drawing

Advantages	Limitations
• Improves accuracy and reduces errors • Increased productivity and saves time • Better quality drawings • Easy to share for collaboration	• Requires skill training • Work prone to viruses and hacking • Work loss due to computer crashing or parts breaking • High purchase cost for new system

Stretch

Designers use a variety of modelling techniques to develop their ideas. This sometimes involves working directly with materials and components in various forms:

- card modelling
- CAD
- virtual modelling
- breadboarding.

Choose one of these modelling techniques. Describe how your chosen modelling technique is used to develop products and give examples.

Review your learning

Test your knowledge   8

1   Can you name two kinds of 2D and two kinds of 3D drawing used in engineering design?

2   Why is orthographic projection used as a standard around the world?

3   Name some standard conventions of orthographic drawings.

4   What are the benefits of using CAD software when producing technical drawings?

What have you learnt?

	See section
• Types of drawing used in engineering.	3.1
• Types of working drawing and their conventions.	3.2
• The benefits of using CAD in engineered drawings.	3.3

Evaluating design ideas

Let's get started

Engineers have ways of evaluating their ideas to determine if they are successful or not.

Have you ever sketched an idea and thought your first idea was your best one? How do you know it's your best idea? How do you know whether to keep trying or stick with the idea you have had?

Figure 1.93: Engineers use several different methods of evaluating design ideas.

What will you learn?

- Methods of evaluating design ideas.
- Modelling methods.
- Methods of evaluating a design outcome.

4.1 Methods of evaluating design ideas

Once you have generated a range of suitable design ideas to meet a brief, just choosing your favourite isn't going to be justification enough to reach a final idea. You are going to have to test the design to create some solid evidence that it is suitable.

When evaluating design ideas you can use a range of methods to help choose the best idea, some more rigorous and technical than others. Some of the common methods to be aware of are:

- production of models
- qualitative comparison with the design brief and specification
- ranking matrices
- quality function deployment (QFD).

Production of models

As mentioned previously, models can be used in many ways to assist in testing a design. Before any physical testing takes place, a designer can use a model to give a client a complete idea of how a product would look in real life.

A model:

- clarifies the product's purpose, function and appearance
- helps designers and engineers better understand the product prior to manufacture
- gives the client a clearer understanding of the processes and costs required to realise the design.

You will have to give some serious thought as to what kind of model will suit your test best. Scale models may not be suitable for evaluating sizes of a product. Models that are specifically designed to test the function might not look enough like the product to evaluate the appearance of the design.

Qualitative comparison with the design brief and specification

Perhaps the most obvious way of evaluating your design is to compare it with the specification. You wrote the specification based on the brief and the research and you designed using it, so it makes sense to check your designs against it.

Engineers use the brief and specification as a checklist to justify if the design is successful. Some of the points are quite subjective. For example, points about a product's aesthetics being attractive are a matter of opinion. For these, the design is often shown to the client, customers or other engineers to gauge opinion.

This process is known as a **qualitative comparison**. It doesn't create exact facts and figures, but is gauging opinion and feeling on a design.

It is particularly useful to ensure:

- the client's requirements are met
- the product's aesthetics are correct
- there are no errors within the design.

Test your knowledge   1

1   Name some methods you can use to evaluate your design ideas.
2   Why is it important to evaluate your design ideas?
3   What is the purpose of physical modelling of your design ideas?

Ranking matrices

Ranking matrices (also called decision matrices) are used as tools to help make decisions when comparing products where more than one option and several factors need to be considered. Often the criteria will be based on your specification.

Types include: simple rank matrix, weighted rank matrix and datum rank matrix.

Simple rank matrix

This is simply scoring your ideas and seeing which idea scores the highest overall. Down the side you need to identify a range of things your design should have or do: the ranking criteria. These can be taken from your specification. You will then score each of your designs against these criteria. You can score them out of 5, out of 10, out of 100 – as long as you use the same grading for all the designs.

Table 1.23: Simple rank matrix

Criteria	Options		
	Car A	Car B	Car C
Cost	5	3	3
Practicality	2	4	3
Performance	4	2	5
Reliability	1	2	4
Fuel economy	2	3	3
Total	**14**	**14**	**18**

In Table 1.23, the car designs have been scored against five criteria by the designer. They have chosen to score each of them out of 5. By scoring each car design against each criteria then totalling the scores, the designer can see that Car C has scored highest overall.

Note that a simple rank matrix assumes that all of your criteria are of equal importance. This is not always the case. For example, reliability and colour of the car are probably not of equal importance.

Weighted rank matrix

Sometimes you will have points that are more important than others. Often the function and suitability of a product are more important than other features. To represent this a weighted rank matrix adds a 'weighting' column that allows you to make some of your criteria worth more points than others.

Table 1.24: Weighted rank matrix

		Options					
		Option 1		Option 2		Option 3	
Criteria	Weighting	Score	Total	Score	Total	Score	Total
Criteria 1	1	1	1	5	5	5	5
Criteria 2	2	2	4	4	8	5	10
Criteria 3	3	3	9	3	9	5	15
Criteria 4	4	4	16	2	8	5	20
Criteria 5	5	5	25	1	5	5	25
Total			55		35		75

When scoring your product against the criteria this time, the score is multiplied by the number in the 'weighting' column. In Table 1.24, each score given for Criteria 5 is worth five times as much as each score given for Criteria 1. Criteria 5 is obviously a much more important feature in your design.

Using the previous simple matrix, Options 1 and 2 would have scored the same points (fifteen each). The ranked matrix recognises that Criteria 5 is more important, so Option 1 scores 55 compared to Option 2 at 35. This makes it harder to work out and read but more sophisticated when making decisions.

Datum rank matrix

A datum rank matrix is a good way of comparing designs against a chosen design and against each other. Effectively it uses criteria as in the previous methods but instead of scoring, you say if each design is better or worse than the control (datum) design.

Table 1.25: Datum rank matrix to compare containers used to make a pencil case

| Criteria | Products (type of pencil case) | | | |
	Screw top	Matchbox	Zip pouch	Clam shell
Easy to get pencils	–	s		+
Holds a lot	–	–		+
Hardwearing	+	+		–
Fits in a bag	–	s	DATUM	s
Looks good	+	–		+
Safe to use	+	+		–
Better (+)	3	1		3
Worse (–)	3	3		2
About the same (s)	0	2		1
Totals	0	–2		1

In Table 1.25, the designer is comparing containers for a pencil case. The zip pouch is the datum product. All of the others are rated as better (+), worse (–) or the same (s) for each criterion. At the bottom the totals are added up and the design with the highest total is the greatest improvement on the original idea.

Test your knowledge 2

1 Name three types of ranking matrix.

2 Why might a weighted rank matrix give more useful results than a simple rank matrix?

3 How might numerical data be useful when justifying your design decisions to the client?

Quality function deployment (QFD)

Quality function deployment (QFD) is another type of matrix, similar to a datum rank matrix. It was developed in Japan as a way to transform the customers' needs and wants into a product design.

The layout of a QFD grid is complicated and time-consuming to create, but follows a similar trend to the other matrix tables. The criteria for a QFD matrix are based on the customers' requirements and preferences. These may be obtained from the original design brief, information the client already holds, and from market research.

Table 1.26: Quality function deployment (QFD) matrix

Correlation matrix	
+ +	Strong positive
+	Positive
–	Negative
– –	Strong negative
	Not correlated

Relationship matrix		
◉	Strong	6
○	Medium	3
△	Weak	1
	No assignment	0

Customer need	Customer importance rating (1 = low, 5 = high)	Percentage of customer importance rating	Design requirement 1	Design requirement 2	Design requirement 3	Design requirement 4	Design requirement 5	Design requirement 6	Design requirement 7	Design requirement 8	Comp 1	Comp 2	Comp 3	Comp 4
			▼	▼	▲	▲	▲	▲	▲	▲				
Customer need 1	1	4%		◉	△		△	△		○	3	2	1	5
Customer need 2	2	8%	○	◉						◉	2	2	1	4
Customer need 3	3	12%				◉	△				5	2	3	2
Customer need 4	3	12%		◉	◉	○		○	◉	○	2	3	5	1
Customer need 5	4	16%	△	◉	◉	○	△	△	○		2	5	4	3
Customer need 6	3	12%	△	△	△	○				◉	1	1	3	1
Customer need 7	4	16%	△	○	◉	◉			◉		2	5	3	3
Customer need 8	5	20%		◉		○	◉	○			5	3	2	4
Importance score			17	105	70	87	38	29	54	54				
Percent of importance			3.75	23.1	15.4	19.2	8.37	6.39	11.9	11.9				

Competitor research

To produce a QFD matrix, you will need a control product to compare the others to. This can just be the first product you review, the industry standard product of this type, or the client's current product of this type.

The matrix has your ACCESS FM headings across the design requirement columns. The customers' needs are used as the row headings.
To complete the table, you rank the products in each category as worse, the same or better than the control product.

QFD matrices are explored in more detail in unit R040.

4.2 Modelling methods

When making models, you can use a wide range of methods. You don't have to be limited to one method. In modern engineering, designers often produce physical models to show to the client and virtual models to test and modify.

Some methods suit some types of product better. As you become more experienced at designing you will have a better idea which models are most suitable depending on the situation.

Some products also require more testing than others due to safety or accuracy concerns.

Virtual (3D CAD)

Virtual models don't require any physical modelling materials or tools at all. All you need is access to a suitable computer and software.

Reproducing a design using 3D software allows it to be viewed from all angles and you can view individual components. The model can be easily shared and sent via computer to others. 3D models can also be animated and their function simulated too.

The obvious downside is that there is no physical model to handle and test. Often in customer focus groups, physical models are used so that the customer can handle the object.

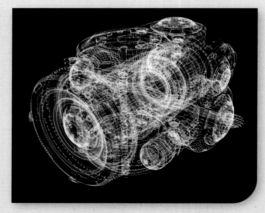

Figure 1.94: A CAD model of an engine

Methods of measuring the dimensions and functionality of the product

As you might imagine, measuring the dimensions of a product is relatively straightforward. You are simply checking the measurements match your original design and are suitable for the brief and specification.

To use measurements to evaluate a design, you will need several things.

- You must have a technical drawing with enough measurements to produce a model.

- Your model must be an accurate reproduction of your technical drawing. It is particularly helpful if your technical drawing states tolerances.

- You must have dimensions you are intending to compare the model to, for example, dimensions provided in the brief or specification or ergonomic data.

Once you have a suitable and accurate model you can use the correct tools to check the sizes.

Table 1.32: Instruments for measuring linear dimensions

Instrument	Description
Rule	<ul><li>Rigid and accurate.</li><li>Used for most linear measurements.</li><li>Normally start their measurements right at the end of the rule (a ruler has a gap before it starts measuring). This makes a rule slightly more useful in measuring into parts and edges.</li></ul>
Vernier callipers	<ul><li>Very accurate.</li><li>Jaws and sliding bar on a set of Vernier callipers are very useful for measuring internal dimensions and depth.</li></ul>
Tape measure	<ul><li>Can measure long distances, so suitable for larger products.</li><li>Flexibility is useful where there is a slight curve or angle involved.</li></ul>
Micrometer	<ul><li>Often accurate to thousandths of a millimetre.</li><li>Constructed of very rigid materials.</li><li>Durable and reliable.</li><li>Require a bit of training and practise to use correctly.</li></ul>
Weigh scales	<ul><li>Can be used to gauge the weight of the product or components (if the models are constructed of the specified materials – there is little point in weighing a foam mock up, for example).</li></ul>

Figure 1.99:
A micrometer screw gauge

For measuring functionality, tests also need to be set. These are often not as simple or accurate as using measuring instruments. Questions that need to be answered when assessing functionality include:

- Does the model do what it is designed to do?
- Is it easy to use?
- How well does the model perform?
- How successful were the features and details?

Quantitative comparison with the design brief and specification

The size and weight measurements gathered can be checked against the product requirements. The original brief and specification will have numerous values and quantities to be met. Checking specific values and numbers, such as size, is a **quantitative comparison**.

Quantitative data is a useful **evaluation** of the product because it is either within the required measurements or not.

This data often helps to determine if:

- the client's technical requirements are met
- the product's dimensions are correct
- the product has the required functions.

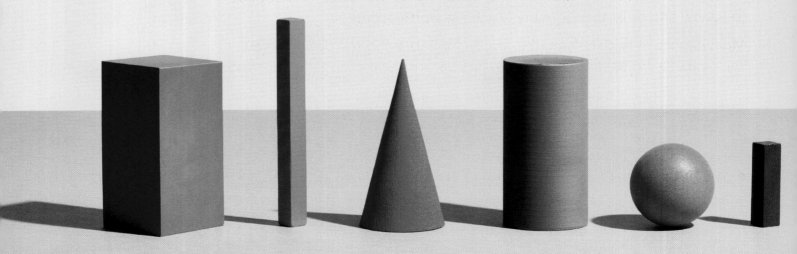

User testing

User testing is a great way to test your design. You might like it but doesn't mean the customer will! Many products have been designed to be successful on paper but have not done well when they have gone to market.

Product testing is carried out by people not related to the designer. Ideally, they would have no prior idea about the designing taking place so their views remain unbiased. They don't share your investment of time and energy in the design. Product testing is also best done with multiple people so you can collect a general overall feel for the views on your product.

Figure 1.100: User testing provides valuable feedback on a product before manufacturing

User testing:

- provides valuable feedback
- helps to identify unforeseen errors or missed opportunities
- allows errors to be corrected before manufacturing begins.

Reasons for identifying potential modifications and improvements to the design

The end goal of creating models and undertaking all this testing is to identify areas that still need improvement. You will have lots of feedback to review and must then identify which are worth acting on.

Most important is identifying the reason for improving the design – you can't extend the development stage just because you changed your mind.

The design may require redesigning if:

- it doesn't meet the function in the brief
- it doesn't meet one or more of the specification points
- the users dislike an aspect of it, such as the aesthetics, size or shape.

To justify the areas identified, you must explain why your design doesn't meet the requirements in these areas. Hopefully, this will also help you to identify how you might improve or alter the design.

Review your learning

Test your knowledge 5

1 Name some ways of evaluating design ideas.
2 What is the difference between virtual and physical modelling?
3 What are the advantages of qualitative and quantitative data?
4 How will a designer use the information generated from the testing and evaluation stages?

What have you learnt?

	See section
• The methods for evaluating design ideas.	4.1
• Different methods of modelling.	4.2
• Different methods of evaluating a design outcome.	4.3

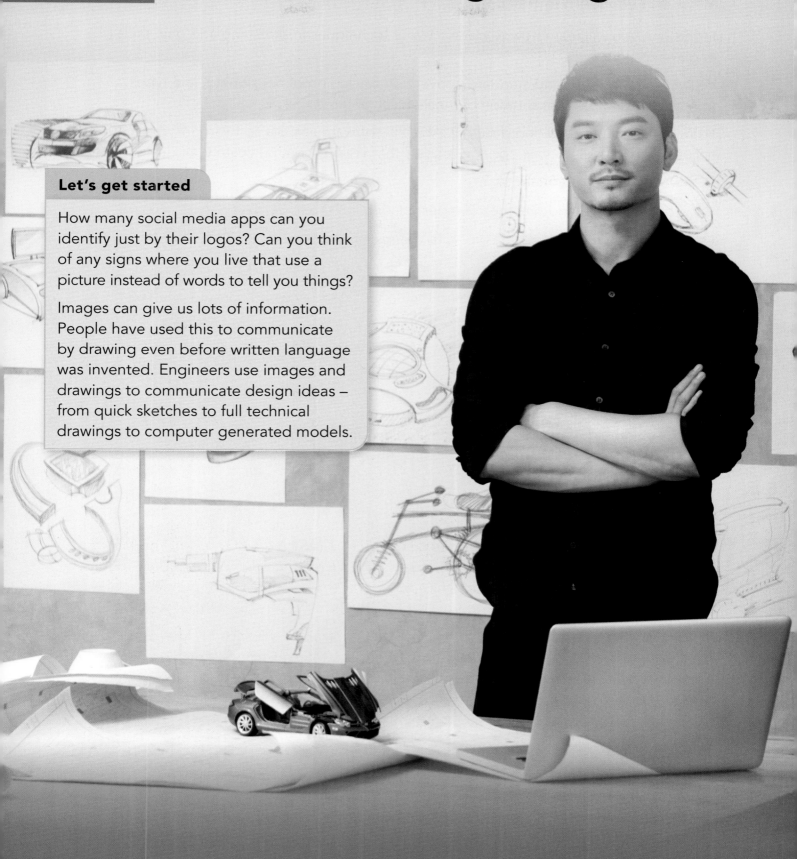

R039 Communicating designs

Let's get started

How many social media apps can you identify just by their logos? Can you think of any signs where you live that use a picture instead of words to tell you things?

Images can give us lots of information. People have used this to communicate by drawing even before written language was invented. Engineers use images and drawings to communicate design ideas – from quick sketches to full technical drawings to computer generated models.

What will you learn in this unit?

In this unit you will learn how to develop your techniques in sketching and gain skills in engineering drawing.

You will learn about using standard conventions including dimensioning, line types, abbreviations and representation of mechanical features.

You will use computer aided design (CAD), 2D software and 3D software to produce accurate and detailed drawings and models that visually communicate your designs.

In this unit you will learn about:

- producing freehand sketches of a design idea in 2D and 3D **TA1**

- producing proposals that respond to the specification provided **TA1**

- developing design proposals with annotation and labelling **TA1**

- producing technical drawings using the correct standards and conventions **TA2**

- using CAD software to produce formal presentation design proposals **TA3**.

How you will be assessed

The marking criteria for this non-exam assessment (NEA) requires you to do a lot of drawing and computer aided design (CAD). You should plan your time accordingly. The work you produce for this NEA is scored out of 60 and will be marked against a mark scheme provided by the exam board. It doesn't take into account any work you have done for other units or produced before or after the NEA.

The total marks are split into 18 marks for sketching and annotating, 12 for developing an idea, 12 for producing technical drawings and 18 for producing a 3D model. For each topic, the examiner will decide if your work matches the low, medium or high level descriptions. Some of these marks are for working independently, so you should aim to produce all work with as little assistance as possible.

If a task or part of a task is missing, it will score no marks and significantly lower your overall mark. Also, be aware, marks are awarded separately for each section (sketching, technical drawing and 3D modelling) so you can't get full marks on the whole unit just by doing 3D modelling, even if the work is excellent. You must ensure you have entered something for all parts of the task.

Manual production of freehand sketches

Let's get started

Have you ever tried to explain something to someone and resorted to a quick drawing on a scrap of paper? Maybe a simple map with directions to somewhere, or showing what something looks like?

Designers use sketching because it is a quick and rough method of recording and explaining ideas.

What will you learn?

- How to produce design sketches of a certain standard and show you can think of a range of design ideas.

- How to draw ideas that meet the brief and specification using drawings and notes to explain the process.

- How to use techniques such as thick/thin lines, shade, tone and texture in your drawings.

- How to use annotations and labels on your sketches, such as sizes, materials and suitability.

- How to explain that your drawings are suitable for the client and/or the customer.

- How to improve drawings by, for example, adding detail and explanation, or clarifying how parts work with more drawings and notes.

- How to produce a range of sketches of one of your developed designs, using different drawing techniques.

- How to add notation to your chosen developed design to explain its features, why they set it apart, how they work and how it meets the design specification.

1.1 Sketches for a design idea

Produce a freehand sketch of a design idea

You will be asked to produce a range of creative sketches. These should all meet the design criteria given in the brief and specification. Drawing a range of ideas that don't meet the requirements will affect your mark, even if they are excellent designs. You must start by re-reading the brief, reviewing your research and making sure you are clear on the requirements.

Freehand sketches can be produced in a range of media. Pencil is a common starting point, but designers often use ink, pencil crayon or marker. Practise with different media and decide which you are most comfortable with. Pencil is easy to erase, but pencil crayon allows better control over the pressure and darkness of lines. You might also try combining more than one material – for example, sketching in pencil then refining lines with fineliner, pencil crayon or both.

2D and 3D sketches

You have been asked to produce both 2D and 3D sketches. A 2D sketch only shows two dimensions of a product – it has no apparent depth. That means you don't need to show the sides of the object you are drawing or any detail on the sides. This doesn't give as much information about the product but is quick to produce.

You don't need tools to produce a sketch. It's okay to work without a ruler. It's a good idea to practise finding a good balance between keeping your sketches quick but also neat enough to understand. Sketches can be done in pencil, pencil crayon or ink so try each medium and decide which you are most comfortable with.

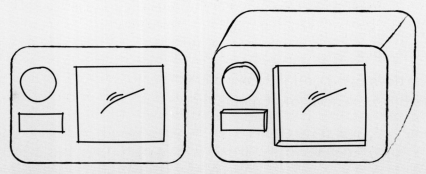

Figure 2.1: Sketching in 2D and using 3D oblique projection

A 3D sketch uses a convention to show the depth of the object you are designing. This is different from a 3D model as the depth is only suggested on the page and the drawing itself is still flat. One of the quickest 3D drawing methods is oblique – the freehand nature of sketching means the inaccuracies of oblique projection don't matter. You can use oblique to extend some of your 2D sketches into 3D.

For high quality outcomes there should be a range of designs and techniques. Remember, they don't need to be accurate, but they do need to be neat and well thought out, otherwise they won't convey the information about your design well.

You are looking to produce a number of possible ideas. If you get stuck, try taking the designs you have already produced and rearranging the same features in a different way: reposition the buttons or alter the shape of the case, for example.

Thick and thin lines

You can use thick and thin lines to give your drawing more impact and give more information about your design. If you use a thick line, it means there is another side attached to that edge that you can't see from this angle. To use thick and thin lines you should follow these rules:

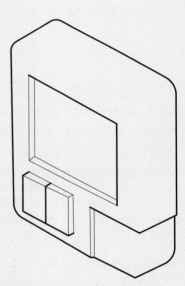

- **Thick lines** are used where only one side or surface can be seen and the joined side is out of sight. On the diagram, the remaining three sides of the shape are hidden from us, so the line around the outside of the design is a thick line. We can't see under the edge of the screen so that is a thick line too.

- **Thin lines** are used where more than one surface or side can be seen joined together in the picture. In Figure 2.2, the lines around the bottom edge of the screen and top edge of the buttons are thin because we can see both parts that connect together.

Figure 2.2: A 3D drawing using thick and thin line convention

Hands on!   1

1   Create a range of sketches in 2D of a digital device with a screen and two buttons. Try varying the design by altering the placement, size and shape of the parts.

2   Use oblique drawing to turn some of your 2D drawings into 3D.

3   Take one of your designs and try to apply thin and thick line convention to it.

Texture

You can add **texture** to your drawing to represent materials and finishes. A variety of drawing materials can be used. You should practise with any materials you intend to use, drawing simple shapes before you attempt a complex design idea.

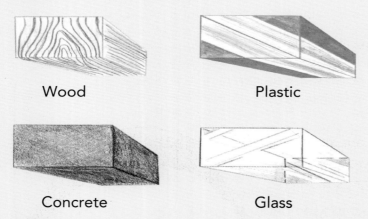

Wood

Plastic

Concrete

Glass

Figure 2.3: Using texture to simulate a range of materials

For natural wood, you can use brown, yellow and orange to draw the wood pattern and end grain. You can then gently colour over the grain lines with yellow or brown.

For plastic, you can use the same colour in stripes of different pressure to suggest a shiny surface. You can also use an eraser to add highlights.

For cement and other rough, grainy materials, you can apply greys in patches and random dots to build up the appearance of a rough texture.

For transparent materials, such as glass and some plastics, you will be able to see through the shape to the hidden edges on the far side. You can make them lighter than the closer edges, or make the lines broken and intermittent.

You can also use marker pens to create texture. Spirit-based pens give a more even finish than water-based ones.

Traditionally, airbrushing was used to add colour to design ideas. Airbrushes spray oil or paint to give a smooth, high-quality finish. It is very easy to accidentally spray the wrong parts of the drawing, though, so you need lots of practice. Use tape or film to mask off areas that are not being sprayed.

Texture is often used in combination with tone, as the way the light hits will make different faces different shades and colours.

Figure 2.4: Airbrushing creates smooth colour and rendering

Tone

When you look at 3D objects – even ones that are all the same colour – some areas appear lighter or darker than others due to the light. These dark and light shades are **tone**.

You can use pencil or pen to create tone in your drawing through several methods.

Pencil shading

You can press harder and lighter with a pencil to create darker and lighter shades. To help you do this, have a range of pencils available. A 5B pencil can make a much darker shade than HB, and a 5H makes a much lighter shade when pressed on.

For fine details, use the point of the pencil at a steep angle. When shading, it's much easier to get a smooth gradient with the edge of the pencil rather than the tip.

Figure 2.5: Ink drawing using cross hatching to show tone

Dots

You can build areas of tone by adding dots of pencil or fineliner. You can add more concentrated areas of dots where the shade would be darker and less where it would be lighter.

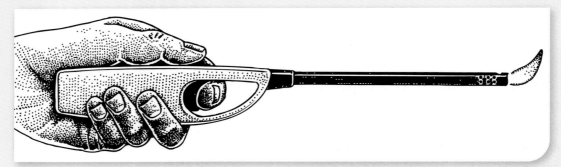

Figure 2.6: Using dots to draw a lighter

Cross hatching

As with the dot technique, you can use cross hatched lines to add shaded areas. Again, use closer, denser lines to represent shade (see Figure 2.5). To make it neat, keep the hatch lines parallel and consistent with each other.

Shading

To create shade you need to start by considering where the light is coming from. If the light is behind the object, you are going to have to draw a lot of shade and shadow. If the light source is coming from your direction you are going to be drawing a lot of highlights.

Shading specifically relates to darkened, shaded areas on your design. If you imagine pointing a lamp at your object, the shadows on the far side of the object and the ground are the areas of shade. As with tone, you need to consider the direction of the light before you start.

Figure 2.7: Using shading

One and two point perspective

Perspective drawing is another method used by graphic designers to give the impression of a 3D shape. The object is drawn getting smaller as it goes into the distance. This represents the way we see things as smaller the further away they are from us.

If you imagine a train coming towards you, the engine and first carriages would appear larger than the ones at the end of the train. To draw in perspective requires you to make dimensions smaller the further away the object is meant to be. Although it may give the illusion of depth to an object, it cannot be considered accurate or technical and you cannot take measurements off it.

One point perspective drawing

In Figure 2.8, the room has been drawn in one point perspective. While the vertical and horizontal lines closest are drawn normally (the X and Y axes), the depth lines are drawn vanishing towards one point on the horizon. The chair in the room would be smaller if it was placed further away from us. All of the lines in this diagram head towards a single vanishing point in the middle of the page that can be just identified as a dot.

Figure 2.8: A room drawn in one point perspective

Two point perspective drawing

In Figure 2.9, the building has been drawn in two point perspective. The vertical lines are still straight (the Y axis) but the X and Z axes recede off to two vanishing points on the horizon at the left and right edge of the image. The effect gives the impression of a 3D object but cannot be measured; the edge of the building in the centre of the page would measure much bigger than the two at the edge of the page, despite being the same in real life.

Figure 2.9: A building drawn in two point perspective

Hands on!   2

1   Sketch a series of six cubes. Render them in a variety of materials. You might try wood, metal, stone, concrete or glass.

2   Add shade and tone to a cube. Shade it as if the light is coming from the top left corner of the page.

3   Attempt to shade and texture a more complicated shape. You could draw a collection of shapes grouped together or attempt to draw an actual product to shade.

Annotation and labelling techniques

Not all details of your design can be communicated with drawing. There may be hidden details, moving parts or pieces that need to be explained. You can write notes that can be read by the person looking at your diagrams. To do this you will need both **annotations** and **labels**.

Annotations are explanatory notes added to give more information or to clarify a detail. In Figure 2.10, the annotation provides size and weight information that couldn't be conveyed through drawing.

Labels name parts to identify them. In Figure 2.10, the entrance of the tent has been labelled so it is clear it is an opening and not just a change in the design of the fabric. For your designs you might want to consider notes and annotations including the following details.

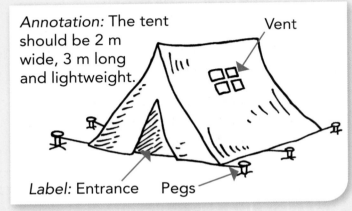

Figure 2.10: A drawing with added labels and an annotation

Key features

The key features on your design are the parts you have added to set it apart from similar products or your other designs. They make your design interesting and hopefully attractive to your target audience.

Some features are electronic, or only reveal themselves when the product is used. They will require annotation to explain them at this stage. For example, you would not be able to show, just by drawing, that an MP3 player design has Wi-Fi.

Your drawings must clearly identify the parts of your design that make it unique. This will help you to make design decisions later on and also convey important information to the client.

Functions

The function of your design is what it does. It's always a good idea to explain the function of a design, even if you think it's obvious from how it looks. Your design *must* meet the function required in the brief, so it is good to make it very obvious that it meets the criteria.

Adding annotations about function is also the perfect opportunity to explain why you think this design is particularly suitable for its function: think about what sets this design apart from the rest.

Dimensions

When sketching, dimensions can be added as annotations. These might be simple size directions, such as 'the tent should be 3000 mm × 2000 mm'.

You might also use comparative sizes in your notes, such as 'the grip is sized for four adult fingers'.

Adding dimension annotations is important when sketching because you haven't used any specific **scale** or drawn proportions accurately, so it's the only way to indicate size.

> Remember, if you are doing any style of technical drawing there will be very specific ways to add dimensions and you will need to use correct drawing conventions for that drawing style.

Materials

Some of your material choices may be apparent from your drawings. You should, however, also add notes to explain your choice of material. These might just be a simple label at this initial design stage, with a general suggestion such as a polymer or a metal.

As your ideas develop this might be a full annotation stating a very specific material and explaining the reasoning behind that material too.

Stretch

Engineering designers must use images and labels to clearly explain their ideas and how they work.

Sketch a design for a desk tidy that would hold a range of stationery items. Annotate it using ACCESS FM so there would be enough information to produce the tidy, even if you took the images away.

Challenge someone else to try to draw what your design looks like by only using the annotations.

Produce an isometric sketch for a design proposal

As mentioned in R038, isometric designs are useful for giving much more information about your design ideas. To help meet the mark scheme, it's a good idea to develop some of the 2D and 3D sketches you produced for the first part of this task. In other words: take the same idea, improve it and refine it.

Your isometric designs can be used to demonstrate all of the techniques mentioned so far: thick and thin line convention, texture, tone and shade. Because they are more accurate and require ruler use, it's a good idea to start to make some size and scale decisions at this point too.

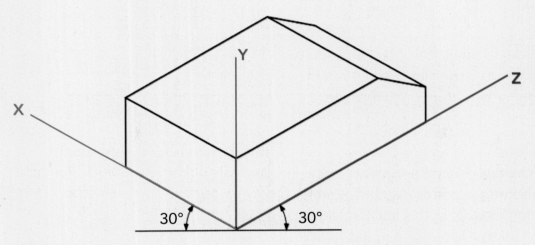

Figure 2.11: Isometric drawing showing the X and Z axes at 30 degrees

Rules of isometric

Isometric drawing allows you to draw and show three sides of your design at the same time. Imagine it like a graph, but with some of the axis going *into* the paper. The X-axis represents the width of the object and is drawn at 30 degrees. The Z-axis represents depth and is drawn at 30 degrees. The Y-axis represents the object's height and is drawn upright, just like a typical 2D drawing. None of the lines is shortened or extended. They can all be drawn actual size or to scale.

Isometric paper

When starting isometric drawing it helps to use isometric layout paper – this has a triangular grid on it representing the X, Y and Z axes. Typically this paper has 10 mm, 5 mm or 1 mm spacing on the grid allowing you to quickly check sizes as you draw. Because the Y-axis is still vertical, you can't turn this paper on its side. In mathematics, isometric paper uses dots to mark out a grid. A dot lies where the X, Y and Z axes meet.

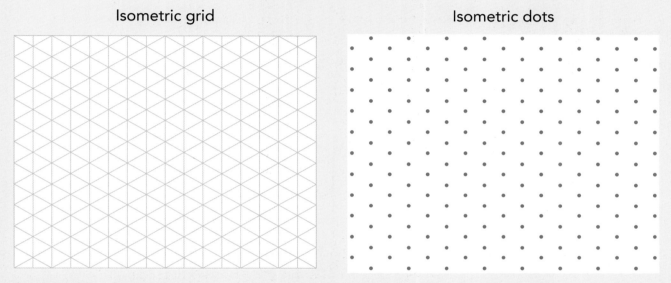

Isometric grid   Isometric dots

Figure 2.12: Isometric layout grids

Getting started drawing isometric

When you start drawing isometric, you need to fool your brain into seeing how the shapes would lie on the three axes. Try drawing simple cubes – start with small cubes, then larger cubes – before trying rectangles and more complex shapes. Aim to use the isometric paper as an underlay and trace through; you might want to start by working directly on the isometric paper.

To help get started, you might try the Y method, the hexagon method, or the book method (see Figure 2.13).

The Y method

Start by drawing a letter Y along the lines. Then outline around the outside of it in a broad hexagon. To draw rectangles, the arms of the Y can be different lengths.

The hexagon method

Start by drawing a hexagon. Add a Y in the middle to complete the cube.

The book method

Start by drawing out an open book shape. To complete the cube, add an inverted V to the top of it.

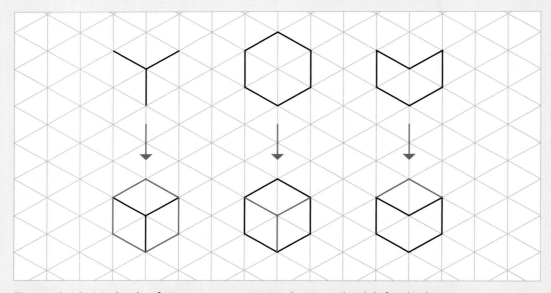

Figure 2.13: Methods of practising isometric: the Y method (left), the hexagon method (centre) and the book method (right)

Hands on!   3

1. Practise drawing simple shapes in isometric. Start with a simple 1 × 1 × 1 cube then try 3 × 3 × 3 and 3 × 2 × 1 until you are familiar with seeing cuboids on isometric paper.

2. Try drawing wedges and curved edges on the side of your cuboids.

3. Try adding shade and texture to one of your isometric shapes.

Beyond cubes

Once you can produce cubes of various sizes, try rectangles, and then arrangements of rectangular shapes and cubes. It helps to think of objects as being made up of a collection of simple shapes – so, for example, a camera might be a rectangle with a cylinder on the front.

Figure 2.14: A cylinder rotated to show distortion

Producing curves and circles in isometric is tricky because, when you look at a disc on an angle, it seems to flatten out and appear as an ellipse. This means you can't just use a compass or a stencil to add a circular shape to an isometric drawing.

To make a circle on your design in isometric you need to mark out a square on the side it is going on. The 'circle' will touch the mid-point of each side of the square, as shown in Figure 2.15. Note this creates an effect where two of the segments curve quite sharply and two of the segments curve in a shallow way, creating an ellipse. To help, draw the square and the mid points very lightly in pencil so you can remove the unwanted lines afterwards.

A good isometric drawing can also use all of the techniques already mentioned to make it more effective. Consider using thick and thin lines, texture, tone and shading on your isometric drawing when aiming for higher marks.

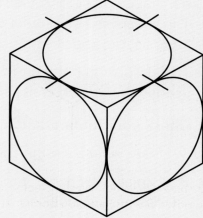

Figure 2.15: Drafting isometric circles by using a square to locate each quarter

Case study

Ingenuity

The Mars helicopter, Ingenuity, was designed and created by NASA. In 2020 it was launched to Mars attached to the underside of the Perseverance rover. After landing on the planet in February 2021, it sought out a suitable lift-off site.

In April 2021, Ingenuity flew over the surface of Mars. It proved flying exploration of Mars was possible and at the same time the helicopter became the first powered flight on Mars.

Figure 2.16: The Mars Ingenuity helicopter was the first powered aircraft on Mars

The Ingenuity helicopter is a good example of a product designed to a specification. It needed to resist space travel, radiation and the impact of landing, the temperature on Mars can reach −150°C and the gravity is only one third of that on Earth. There was also no chance of altering the design once it had left the planet and no way of making repairs. This meant the engineers designing the Ingenuity helicopter had to design to a very complicated specification and the design had to perfectly fulfil the design brief.

To help design it the engineers did have one advantage: they could draw upon technology used in unmanned crafts and drones already in use on Earth and build upon this.

Check your understanding

1   State what a design specification is.

2   Explain why it was important for the engineers of the Ingenuity helicopter to create designs that fulfilled the specification.

3   Justify why creating a range of designs and models would have increased the chance of creating a successful product.

Review your learning

Test your knowledge

1　What is the purpose of a sketch drawing?

2　Explain the difference between an annotation and a label.

3　Describe what drawing techniques can be added to a sketch.

4　Explain the conventions of isometric drawing.

What have you learnt?

	See section
• How to use the brief and specification when designing.	1.1
• How to generate design ideas in 2D and 3D.	1.1
• How to use thick and thin lines, texture, tone and shade.	1.1
• How to use annotation and labelling referring to the specification and brief.	1.1
• How to develop one or more ideas using further drawings, isometric and labelling.	1.1
• How to explain how a design is suitable for the client and/or customer.	1.1

TA2

Manual production of engineering drawings

Let's get started

Have you ever seen the characters in a film with a blueprint for a device? Or seen an architect's plan for a house or an extension? What sort of information do you imagine is on them?

Engineers produce technical drawings to impart accurate information about their designs.

What will you learn?

- How to produce an orthographic drawing and the engineering rules for it.

- How to produce drawings that show the parts involved in your design and how they fit together.

- How to produce engineering drawings independently.

2.1 Drawings for a design idea

Once you have completed your sketches, you will need to define all the little details and dimensions and ways it fits together. This involves working in a more accurate way than the sketch stages. You need to think carefully about accuracy and neatness. Measuring tools such as rulers, set squares and compass are essential for this task.

Engineered drawings have very specific rules and methods for drawing and laying out. These are called standard conventions.

Third angle orthographic projection drawing using standard conventions

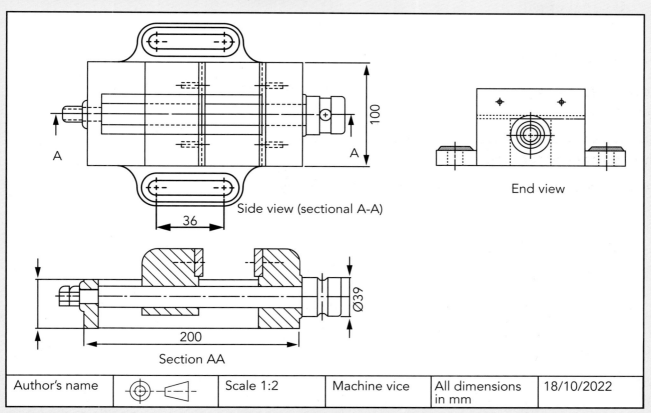

Figure 2.17: A third angle orthographic projection drawing of a product

Orthographic drawing has many rules to it but isn't tricky once you have learnt how it needs to be drawn. **Orthographic projection** is drawing a design in two dimensions, but drawing from enough angles that it provides all of the information required to make it. Usually, this means creating three views: the front view, the plan view and the top view. Arranging these views in a particular order is called third angle. Figure 2.18 shows the information that orthographic drawings must display.

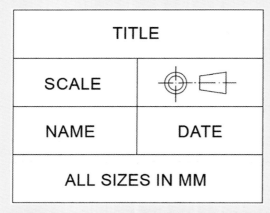

TITLE	
SCALE	⊕⊏
NAME	DATE
ALL SIZES IN MM	

Figure 2.18: The information that all orthographic drawings must display

Orthographic drawing has a set of standard conventions (these are essentially drawing rules), produced by the British Standards Institution (BSI). This means all designers and engineers using orthographic projection create the drawing in the same way and this helps manufacturers and other engineers to read each other's designs easily. These rules include the layout, title, scale, dimensions and the lines used on the diagrams.

Standard conventions

Layout

You will need to consider the correct layout for your design. Usually, the side that has the most detail will be the front, as you want to be sure to tell the manufacturer about these details.

In some situations, the shape and proportions of the design will dictate a suitable layout. In Figure 2.19, neither of the arrangements is necessarily wrong. However, the second option clearly fits better and keeps the designs close and relatable to each other.

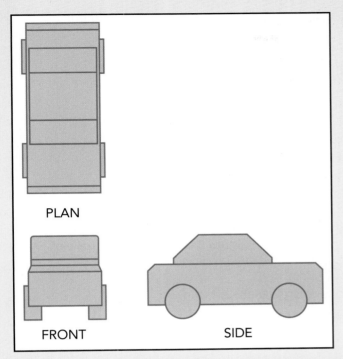

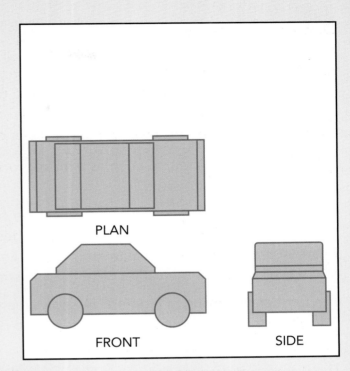

Figure 2.19: Two possible third angle layouts for the same design

Note each angle of the drawing is perfectly in line with the other views. They are also exactly the same size. This is very important in orthographic drawing.

Title

You will need a 10mm border around your drawing and a title block at the bottom of your drawing. This can either be a block set in the bottom right corner or a strip across the bottom.

You will need to add your name, the third angle orthographic symbol, the drawing title, the scale to which it is drawn, what units the measurements are in and the date (see Figure 2.20).

NAME	⊕⊟	SCALE	TITLE	ALL SIZES IN MM	DATE

Figure 2.20: A title block running along the bottom of the page

Scale

Orthographic drawings are accurate. You need to indicate the scale you have drawn in. If the product is small, such as a pair of earbud headphones, you might be able to draw the design actual size – this is 1:1 and makes creating the drawing simple. If you are drawing larger products, such as a bike, or smaller products, such as a microprocessor, you need to draw them to scale.

On the cross design shown in Figure 2.21, the cross in the middle represents the actual size of the final design. Each 1 mm on the drawing represents 1 mm of the final product, so it would be made the same size as this illustration.

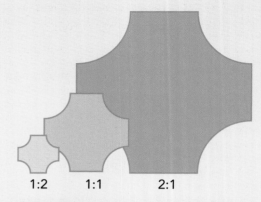

Figure 2.21: Altering the scale of a drawing

The left-hand drawing in Figure 2.21 shows the cross redrawn at half its actual size (scale 1:2). Here, each 1 mm on the drawing represents 2 mm on the product in real life.

The right-hand drawing in Figure 2.21 shows the cross drawn at twice its actual size (scale 2:1). Here, each 1 mm on the drawing represents 0.5 mm in real life.

This means that, when made, all three of these products would be an identical size – changing the scale of a drawing just alters how big or small the drawing is. It doesn't affect the size of the object in real life. This is very useful when designing bridges or skyscrapers without using massive pieces of paper.

Dimensions

Dimensions are marked in millimetres (mm) on the orthographic drawing. You should also mention this in the title block. You should aim to dimension all parts of your drawing. Lots of dimension arrows can make your drawing very busy and difficult to read. To avoid this, remember that:

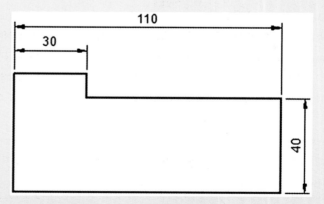

Figure 2.22: Dimension lines added to a simple shape

- dimensions should be given on the outside of your product, not floating inside it

- dimension lines are thinner than the lines used to draw the product – this stops them getting confused with the design

- you don't need to mark the same dimension more than once – so, for example, don't put the width on both the front and plan views, as it is the same dimension twice.

As mentioned previously, dimension lines have projection lines that don't quite touch your drawing and filled in arrow heads that do touch the projection lines.

Your dimensions are written in millimetres. If your drawing is actual size, that's the size on the paper. If it's to scale, the dimension values will show the size of the actual product, not the size of the drawing on the paper.

Test your knowledge   1

1. State what three views are presented in third angle orthographic drawing.
2. What units are normally used to present a third angle drawing?
3. Explain the standard conventions used in setting up a third angle drawing.

Hands on!   1

1. Draw a 10 mm border around a page and add a title block.
2. Draw a cuboid 60 mm × 30 mm × 20 mm in orthographic projection on your paper.
3. Add a size dimension arrow to one part of the diagram.

Produce an assembly drawing for a design proposal

Assembly drawings contain all the important manufacturing information required to make your design. They are 3D drawings and you may end up producing several types to explain your design in detail. They are a combination of technical drawings and a list of the parts needed to produce the design.

Isometric projection

Isometric projection can be used to create 3D sectional views, exploded diagrams and assembly drawings of your design. As when drawing the outside of a product, isometric is an accurate drawing style and allows you to see three sides of your design neatly rendered.

Sectional views

You can use a cross-sectional isometric where you want to explain how the inside of the product or a component appears. This is especially useful when the product is hollow and contains components. The sectional view in Figure 2.23 allows us to see the design contains a hole that runs completely through it and that the surrounding component is otherwise solid.

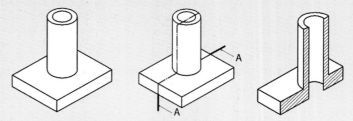

Figure 2.23: Generation of a cross-sectional isometric drawing

Exploded views

Exploded views show how a part of your design fits together. In Figure 2.24, it shows how the fixings line up passing through both sheets of material.

These views are often used by flat packed furniture companies to explain how to assemble their products as they are very simple to understand with little chance of confusion.

To make an exploded view, you may wish to draw the complete part in isometric first and then trace over it, spacing out the parts as you do so, before filling in the blanks. Notice also the use of a centre line, which helps explain the assembly and also keeps all the components in perfect isometric with each other.

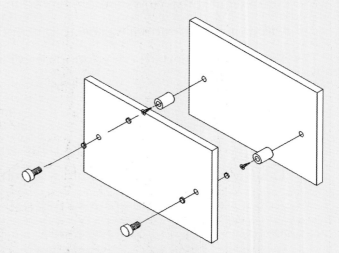

Figure 2.24: An isometric exploded view

Assembly views

Assembly views are a more complex version of an exploded diagram. An assembly view shows how all parts involved in the product fit together though, not just one section. This can make assembly drawings very busy diagrams, so it is important to be neat and use correct line conventions.

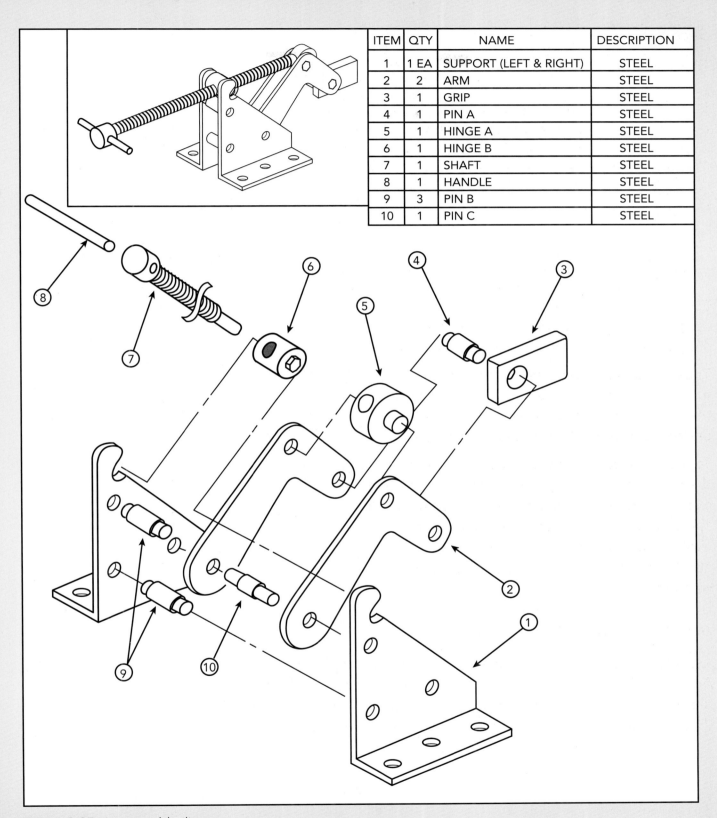

ITEM	QTY	NAME	DESCRIPTION
1	1 EA	SUPPORT (LEFT & RIGHT)	STEEL
2	2	ARM	STEEL
3	1	GRIP	STEEL
4	1	PIN A	STEEL
5	1	HINGE A	STEEL
6	1	HINGE B	STEEL
7	1	SHAFT	STEEL
8	1	HANDLE	STEEL
9	3	PIN B	STEEL
10	1	PIN C	STEEL

Figure 2.25: An assembly diagram

1   Disassemble a pen. Lay out all of the parts in order and draw an exploded view of the pen in isometric.

2   Draw a centre line running through the parts to show how they fit together.

Centre line

On the assembly drawing, centre lines have been added. These add detail to show how the product fits together. The lines show how the parts fit into the holes. In Figure 2.26 the centre line on the part labelled 10 shows it passing through the holes in the two adjacent bars.

When you draw centre lines, remember correct line convention and be careful to align all the parts that should fit together. The easiest way to do this is to measure and use the isometric paper as a guide.

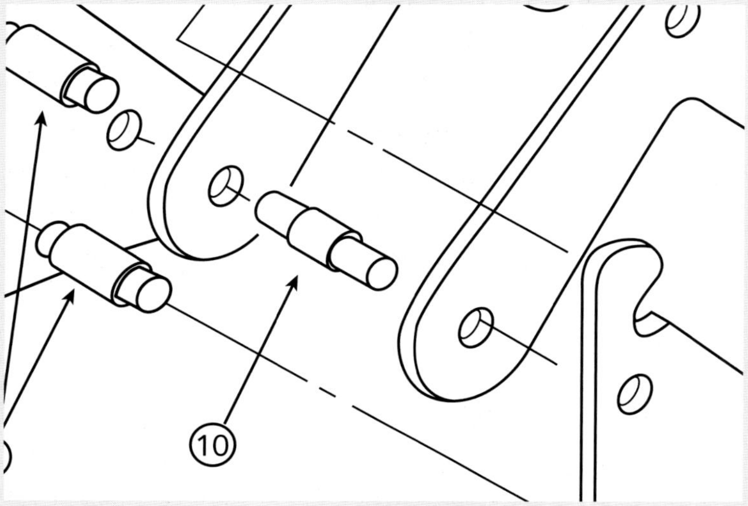

Figure 2.26: Close up of assembly drawing showing centre lines

Parts list

Your diagram should include a parts list of all parts required to manufacture the product (Figure 2.27). Typically, this will name each part of the assembly and give an indication of material. You may also specify dimensions and thickness here.

ITEM	QTY	NAME	DESCRIPTION
1	1 EA	SUPPORT (LEFT & RIGHT)	STEEL
2	2	ARM	STEEL
3	1	GRIP	STEEL
4	1	PIN A	STEEL
5	1	HINGE A	STEEL
6	1	HINGE B	STEEL
7	1	SHAFT	STEEL
8	1	HANDLE	STEEL
9	3	PIN B	STEEL
10	1	PIN C	STEEL

Figure 2.27: Parts list on an assembly drawing

Parts number referencing

For clarity, the individual parts can be numbered on the parts list and the assembly diagram. This allows the reader to quickly identify each part and reference the technical details associated with it.

Assembly instructions

It is also good practice at this stage to identify any assembly methods required to put the parts together. As the engineer, you are designing products that are likely to be produced by a manufacturer and in varying quantities. This means your design must be detailed enough that someone else can take it away and make it without your intervention.

You may choose to add notes on the diagrams themselves or write a separate set of instructions on how to put it together. For products with numerous parts, this might have several stages. You may wish to supplement the instructions with a flowchart or further diagrams.

Case study

Wembley Stadium

Wembley Stadium was rebuilt in 2007 to increase its capacity and modernise the building. The new Wembley Stadium can seat 90 000 people, making it the biggest sports venue in the UK.

The Wembley arch is 133 metres high and supports the large canopy roof. It was designed by Sir Norman Foster. It is the largest single-span roof structure in the world. It means there is no need for pillars inside the structure, enabling every seat to get a clear view to the pitch.

Figure 2.28: The Wembley arch above Wembley Stadium

Sketching played an early role in visualising the iconic design that had to replace the previous Wembley towers. Sketching alone, however, could not prove the design would be suitable, strong enough or safe enough to be viable. The weight of the spectators would place five-and-a-half million kilograms of weight on the structure. Adding the factors of movement, equipment, supplies and weather, the engineers had to be confident that the design would be up to the task.

Continued

The designers of the stadium also needed to ensure that the design was strong enough to support all of these enormous pressures but at the same time remain light enough to be possible. Technical drawings, calculations and detailed planning allowed the engineering team to ensure the building would be safe and fit for purpose.

Check your understanding

1   State why sketching alone would not be suitable to design an engineered project such as a football stadium.

2   Explain what sort of technical details would be found on the technical drawings of a football stadium.

3   Justify why making a structure like this might take significantly longer and cost more money without comprehensive technical drawings.

Stretch

Engineers produce technical drawings of products to explain them. They use cutaway and cross-sectional diagrams to explain what is happening inside the product.

Get a cheap bike light. Using measuring instruments and a ruler, draw your bike light in orthographic projection using a scale of 2:1.

Carefully take apart the bike light. Use the opened product to turn one view of your drawing into a cross-sectional diagram.

Review your learning

Test your knowledge   2

1   State what information must go on a title block.

2   Explain what a sectional view shows on a diagram.

3   Explain what information can be gained from an assembly view.

4   Justify the need for accurate engineered drawings. What would happen if they were not present?

What have you learnt?

	See section
• How to create an orthographic drawing.	2.1
• How to use the correct rules and conventions including layout, title, scale, line convention and dimensions.	2.1
• How to create a sectional view of part of a product.	2.1
• How to create exploded and assembly drawings for a design.	2.1
• How to create a parts list and use a numbering system identifying the parts.	2.1
• How to create assembly instructions for a design.	2.1

TA3

Use of computer aided design (CAD)

Let's get started

If you have ever played 3D games on a computer or games console, you'll know how immersive it is to be able to move and look around a 3D environment, compared with a flat platform game.

What will you learn?

- How to create a complex 3D model using CAD software of a chosen design.

- How to create a detailed model made up of numerous individual parts, all 3D modelled (that is, not just one shape/piece).

- How to produce CAD models without help – so you need to be familiar and confident using CAD software before you begin.

3.1 Produce a 3D CAD model of a design proposal to include compound 3D shapes

Computer aided design (CAD) is used in all areas of design and engineering. It enables the creation of complex 3D models of design proposals that can be manipulated and shared without the need for manufacturing. CAD software is intuitive and enables you to create design proposals swiftly and accurately.

You will need to be familiar with the software before attempting the non-exam assessment (NEA). However, there isn't time to learn it as part of the exam and it isn't expected that you should have to learn it in the assessment time. You are advised to practise and attempt several design briefs beforehand. The more familiar you are with the software, the better the outcome. It should after all be a test of your engineering and designing skills, not how well you have learnt to use a piece of software.

There are numerous 3D CAD programs suitable for engineering design. Most have common features, as shown in Figure 2.29.

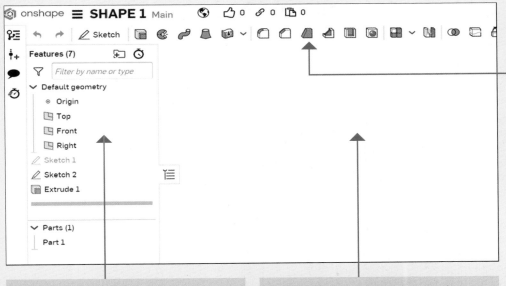

Feature toolbar: Header or sidebar dedicated to tools you can use to generate or manipulate shapes. This is similar in many ways to the toolbar in traditional painting packages. Some packages have multiple toolbars to select between.

History and drawing detail: Sidebar listing the various parts you are working with and have been working with. This helps organise your design especially where it is made up of multiple components.

Drawing area: Similar to regular paint packages, one or more windows where the active design can be worked on and manipulated. The drawing area is the main workspace of the CAD program.

Figure 2.29: A 3D CAD software screen

Produce a 3D CAD model of a design proposal to include compound 3D shapes

CAD reference geometry

Work planes

CAD software works on three axes: X, Y and Z. As with isometric these are like the axes of a graph: X going left to right, Y going bottom to top and Z going into the page. Because you can rotate a 3D shape, though, the axes are sometimes harder to identify if you have turned the design and are looking at it from underneath, for example.

A **work plane** is like a slice through one of those axes, from the front, the side or the top. When you are working on your design you will often only be working on one work plane at a time, e.g. adding buttons and dials to the front of the design means you only need to work on the one side. The three planes make it a little easier to visualise where on your model you are working.

To get familiar with this, open your CAD software and draw two dimensional shapes or lines in each work plane.

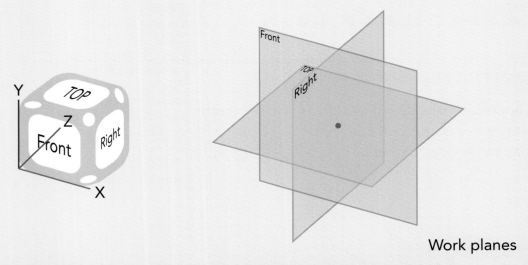

Work planes

Figure 2.30: The three axes used in CAD and the corresponding work planes

CAD sketch tool features

Lines, arcs and polygons

Your 3D software will have sketch tools, very similar to a painting package. These will include lines, curves or arcs and basic shape tools such as rectangles and polygons. These allow you to draw out flat outlines of components before making them 3D. Imagine drawing an object's shadow or footprint.

It is important to remember at this point that 'sketching' in CAD software means producing these flat 2D shapes but it doesn't mean these shapes are inaccurate or rough as it might imply when drawing. Your CAD sketches can be made extremely accurate to specific dimensions.

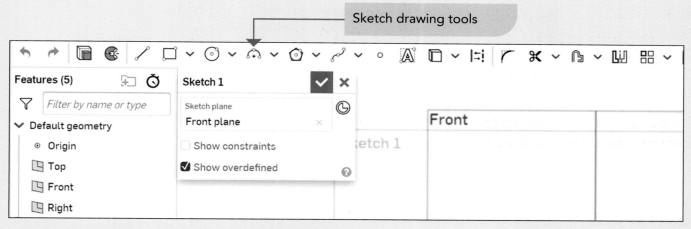

Figure 2.31: Sketch drawing tools on a typical CAD program

All of these sketch tools are effectively 2D – they don't have any depth, so are not a real object yet. Every object needs depth. Even a pencil mark or piece of paper has some depth, so couldn't be manufactured or printed as it is.

Extrudes

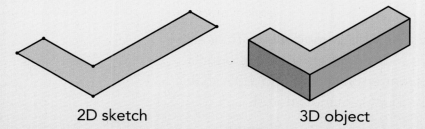

2D sketch   3D object

Figure 2.32: Extruding a sketch into a 3D object

Most CAD software has an **extrude tool**. The extrude tool is possibly the most useful and often used. It can be used to drag an object into 3D. To use it, you will usually create a sketch on a plane using the sketch tools then use the extrude tool to 'drag' the sketch up into 3D. This is effectively adding extra material to the shape to make it taller. It can also be used to make an object thinner again.

Revolves

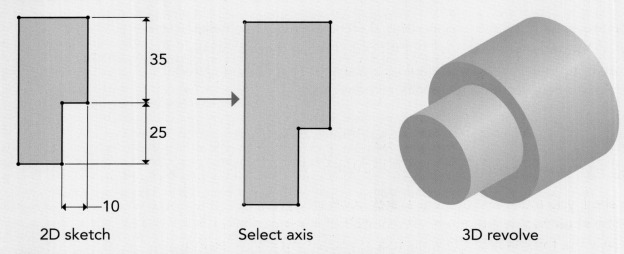

2D sketch   Select axis   3D revolve

Figure 2.33: Converting a 2D sketch into a 3D shape with the revolve tool

The **revolve tool** works in a slightly different way. Instead of stretching a shape up and adding depth to it, it rotates the 2D shape around a point to create a 3D shape. If you drew a circle, for instance, and revolved it around its centre, it would create a sphere.

In the example shown in Figure 2.33 the shape is repeated and revolved around the left-hand edge over and over, creating the 'T' shaped component on the right.

Revolve is particularly useful for creating shaped, tubular components, such as the body of a torch or the axle of a machine.

Sizing and dimensioning

Size and dimension tools are very important in CAD **modelling**. They allow you to accurately input dimensions of your design. Engineered products that are designed 'by eye' will have inherent errors in size and scale that will cause problems later on when the product is manufactured.

Displaying size information also communicates this to the client or manufacturers when exporting images of your design.

Shelling

Shells are used a lot in designing 3D models. Often you want to put something inside a shape: electronic components inside a radio, for example. Creating a shell of a part hollows it out for purposes such as this.

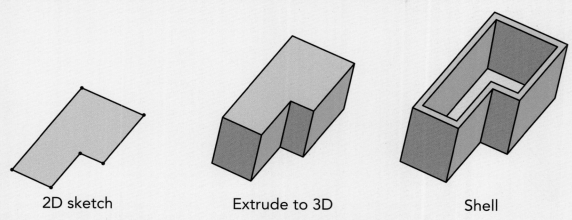

| 2D sketch | Extrude to 3D | Shell |

Figure 2.34: Creating a shell using the extrude and shell tools

To create a shell, you much first use the sketch tools and extrude a 3D shape. The **shell tool** will then enable you to hollow your design. You can specify the thickness of the walls too. If you are making a casing for a product remember you will still need a lid for the extruded shape and will need to model how the parts assemble together.

Holes

Holes are used frequently in CAD modelling, to create connection points for other components or for screws or bolts to go through. They might also allow buttons, screens or cables to fit into a design, or create grips.

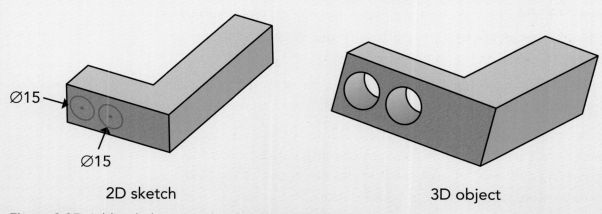

Ø15
Ø15

| 2D sketch | 3D object |

Figure 2.35: Adding holes using sketch and extrude tools

Some CAD software has a dedicated hole tool. Otherwise, the easiest way to create holes is to use the extrude tool again. Sketch the shape of the hole on the side where you wish it to be and then extrude it though the part until it is a hole. You can control the size of the holes accurately by ensuring the sketch dimensions are accurate before extruding.

CAD rendering

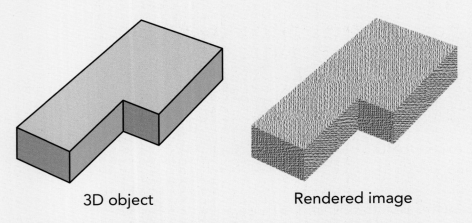

3D object   Rendered image

Figure 2.36: A texture render being applied to a simple shape

Rendering an object in CAD is a lot like rendering an object when drawing, adding texture and light or shadow effects. The ability of a CAD program to create rendering effects varies a lot from software to software. Designers often export their design and use alternative rendering software to get the desired effect.

Rendering an object can add an impression of how the finished design might look in the selected materials or how it might appear in the location where it will be used. Renders are useful if the design needs to be shown to a client or user for their opinion as they make it easier to visualise the product. Rendered images are often exported for use in presentations or promotional material.

By adding material effects to your CAD model, you can attempt to explain how the design might appear and help justify the choice of materials to be used.

Stretch

Engineers use CAD to generate models of their designs and easily test changes to their ideas.

Find a travel mug. Use 3D modelling software to create a 3D copy of the mug, using measuring instruments to ensure accurate dimensions. Modify the CAD object by adding a handle or grip in a suitable size for a twelve-year-old.

Use screen grabs of your design and annotations to create a one-page presentation, explaining what modification you have made.

Produce 3D CAD assemblies of components

CAD models are typically made of many parts. If you imagine producing a CAD model of a rocket or a motorbike, it isn't manufactured from one piece. These products involve hundreds or even thousands of pieces assembled together in the correct sequence.

A good CAD model works in the same way. The model isn't one solid shape – it consists of lots of shapes made separately and put together in the correct place and orientation. If you were designing a skateboard, for instance, you would model the wheels, bearings, bolts, trucks and deck as separate parts and then put these parts together to create the 3D model.

This is also a useful way of working when discussing manufacturing, as each part can be considered and looked at individually.

Aspects of CAD assembly

Multiple components

While it is very useful to have the file of each individual part of your CAD model, there are advantages to putting all the parts together. You can check they fit together, make sure parts that need to be tight are the correct size and you can also view the product as a whole to ensure it matches the original design requirements.

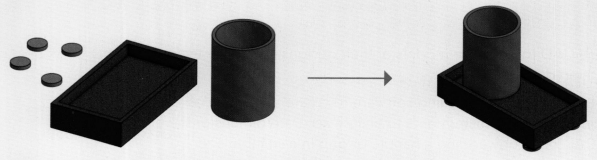

Figure 2.37: Designed components viewed separately and assembled

You can only assemble the components if they are all drawn to the same scale. Good sketches and engineered drawings will help you to ensure that you have enough sizes to work to. Trying to rescale parts by eye afterwards can result in some very strange and unusual measurements that could cause problems later in manufacturing.

Mate and constraint tools

The mate and constraint tools on CAD software allow you to attach your components to each other. The constraint tool allows you to specify the plane on which you want to attach parts together, e.g. ensuring the model of an aerial attaches only to the top of a radio design.

Attaching parts together in this way isn't permanent. You can still access each part if you need specific information.

Animation

Animation is often used in CAD software to simulate how a product might work or move. If your CAD model has moving parts you could record the parts moving to assess the product's **mechanical performance**.

Animation can also be used for aesthetic purposes: recording the 3D model in rotation or in a setting, for example, to demonstrate or present it to interested parties.

Another possible use of animation is to aid assembly by creating an animation where the product components disassemble into an exploded view.

Not all CAD software has animation functions, so you may consider exporting the model to an alternative software or just using a screen recording tool to record as you manually move the necessary parts.

Case study

Virtual windfarms

Windfarms have become a common sight throughout the landscape and coastlines of the UK. By the start of 2022, there were more than 11 000 turbines installed. Turbines cost millions of pounds each and the process of siting them is a complicated and scientific one.

Engineering companies in the UK use 3D modelling to help in the planning and

Figure 2.38: Windfarms are often modelled in 3D

development of offshore windfarms. Virtual models can be generated of coastlines, the sea bed, and of the turbines and cables themselves.

When planning a new windfarm site, from these individual models, the company develops a 3D model of the entire area with the proposed turbines in place. This model is used in several ways:

* The designs can be shown to interested clients and invested parties. They are used in conjunction with virtual reality headsets and allow invested parties to view the site from various places, such as local beaches and towns.

* The designs can quickly generate a cost for the project, including the cost of laying the cables in the water and across land. The models can create an estimate of the energy production of the windfarm.

Check your understanding

1   Wind turbines convert the power of the wind into electricity by turning blades. The shape, size and material of the blades affect the efficiency of the turbine. How might 3D modelling help in the optimisation of the design?

2   The planning and siting of a wind farm is a complicated procedure. Can you think of objections different groups of people might have to the building of an offshore wind farm? You could consider: Environmental agencies, the company requesting the wind farm, investors and local residents.

3   Describe how a 3D model can be used to present the wind farm and develop it so it is acceptable to the client.

Review your learning

Test your knowledge

1   State two advantages of using CAD for modelling.

2   Explain why shelling could be an important tool when designing a radio.

3   Justify the use of rendering on a 3D model.

What have you learnt?

	See section
• How to create a 3D model using CAD software.	3.1
• How to make a model complex in design.	3.1
• How to create multiple separate parts for a design.	3.1
• How to record and present a design for submission.	3.1

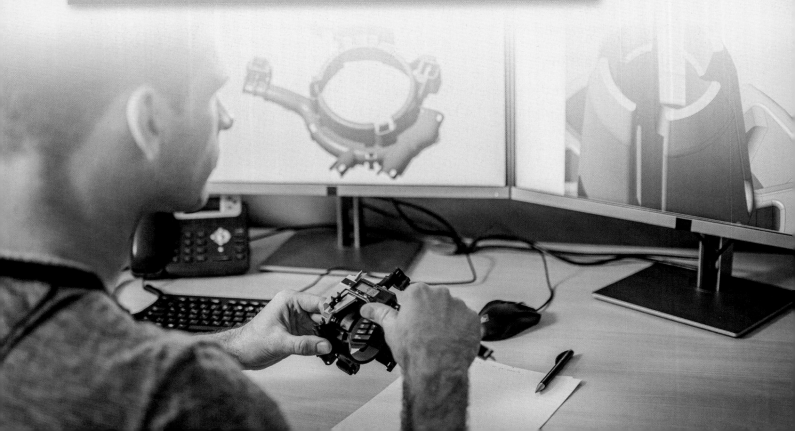

Design, evaluation and modelling

Let's get started

Have you watched programmes where entrepreneurs present their ideas for new products to investors? They show an example of what their products will look like or how it works to convince them of the idea.

A similar thing happens in the engineering world. Engineering designers produce models of improved products, sometimes to show how they look, sometimes to explain how they work.

What will you learn in this unit?

You will learn how designers can quickly create and test models to develop a working prototype of a design. You will develop your virtual modelling skills using computer aided design (CAD) 3D software, to produce a high-quality model that will be able to simulate your design prototype.

You will also develop your physical modelling skills using modelling materials and/or rapid-prototyping processes to produce a physical prototype.

In this unit you will learn about:

- using ACCESS FM to analyse and compare products using an appropriate customer-driven engineering matrix **TA1**

- using primary and secondary research to identify the strengths and weaknesses of existing products **TA1**

- undertaking product research in order to analyse how products are made and assembled **TA1**

- producing a virtual 3D model from a product specification provided **TA2**

- planning the production of a prototype including risk assessments **TA2**

- producing a prototype and recording the process **TA2**

- evaluating your manufactured prototype **TA2**.

How you will be assessed

The marking criteria for this non-exam assessment (NEA) require you to demonstrate skills in product analysis and modelling. The work you produce for this NEA is scored out of 60 and will be marked against a mark scheme provided by the exam board. It doesn't take into account any work you have done for other units or produced before or after the NEA.

The 60 marks are split into 9 marks for analysing existing products, 9 marks for disassembly of a product, 12 marks for 3D modelling of a product idea, 6 marks for planning the production of a prototype, 18 marks for physical modelling of the product and 6 marks for evaluating your prototype. Some of these marks are for working independently, so you should aim to produce all work with as little assistance as possible.

If a task or part of a task is missing, it will score no marks and significantly lower your overall mark. Also, be aware that marks are awarded separately for each section (analysis, disassembly, 3D modelling, planning, production and evaluation) so you can't get full marks on the whole unit just by doing physical modelling without any planning. You must ensure you have entered something for all the parts of the task.

Product evaluation

Let's get started

When you last looked to buy a new computer, games console or phone how did you decide which one to buy? Did you look at customer reviews? Did you research the specifications of several products? Did you go somewhere you could try the products? What eventually made the final decision for you?

Designers analysing existing products must develop fair, rigorous ways to identify good product features and compare products.

What will you learn?

- How to produce a comprehensive product analysis of the key features of products using ACCESS FM.

- How to provide a comprehensive description of the strengths and weaknesses of existing products.

- How to effectively use an engineering matrix.

1.1 Product analysis

To carry out a thorough product analysis, you will have to undertake both **primary** and **secondary research**. You should aim to analyse more than one similar product as this will allow you to compare them. Through the research you are aiming to identify and record the advantages and disadvantages of these products. This will give you the information required to produce your own, hopefully superior, design.

Figure 3.1: Focus groups are a type of primary research used to aid product analysis

Carry out product analysis using ACCESS FM

Product analysis is one of the best sources of information. Whether a success or failure, products on the market have a tried and tested history and a relationship with your target market. A successful product analysis is one that gives you useful information to help you improve your design. You should consider the following.

- Both positives and negatives about a product; ideas you wish to emulate or build upon are just as important as opportunities you identify to improve on. All products will have some positive features – they wouldn't still be in circulation otherwise.

- The product from the point of view of the client; they have a reputation to uphold but also have to make a profit. They also have a brand that this product impacts upon.

- The product from the point of view of the customer/end user. How might they view aspects of this product differently to you? How might their needs and wants be different?

As when you are writing a specification, you can use ACCESS FM to ensure you have a good spread of points and have considered the product from many different perspectives.

Aesthetics

In general you are aiming to explain what the design looks like. Try to explain any themes or trends used in the design. Often designs reflect the style of when or where they were made. The teapot in Figure 3.2 clearly reflects the cultural influences of its country of origin. You could comment on what shape, proportions, colours and textures have been used.

Figure 3.2: A traditional tea set from Marrakesh

To extend on this point you can try to explain why those choices were made by the designer. Objects are often designed to fit in with a brand or range and this influences the design appearance. Sometimes apparently aesthetic features may actually be functional. Texture effects, for example, can add grip to an object.

Cost

For cost, you are looking to explain all aspects of cost related to the product. It isn't enough to just state how much the product is being sold for, though this is a good starting point. High prices can often add status to a product. Dishes in fine dining restaurants command a high price point that helps to reinforce the impression of quality and exclusivity.

Figure 3.3: The high price of fine dining makes it feel even more exclusive

You should extend your answer by considering the price in comparison to similar products. You could research if this is a typical or particularly expensive model of this product. If it is cheap or expensive you could try to justify why. You can also consider the cost to the manufacturer compared with the price paid by the customer and think about profit.

You could try to explain if the price of the product affects its popularity or affordability and if it affects people's perception of the product. Customers often associate cheap with low quality but also want to feel that they have got value for money.

Customer

For customer, you are trying to define who the intended user is. Remember the customer is not always the same as the end user. A child's toy is used by an infant but would be bought by a parent, for example.

To extend your answer you should explain how the design suits their needs. You could try to explain why they would like this product. You could analyse how their particular needs have been addressed.

Figure 3.4: The customer who buys the product is not always the one who uses it

Environment

For environment, you are considering where the product is intended to be used and its impact on the environment. You should consider if it is fit for purpose and how it may have been designed with the environment in mind. In Figure 3.4 for example, all of the products are made using sustainable alternatives to plastic, reducing the need for fossil fuels and the pollution involved.

To extend your answer, you should explain how the 6Rs have been considered (see Table 3.1).

Figure 3.5: Products using non-plastic alternatives

Table 3.1: The 6Rs

6Rs	Consideration
Reduce	Has it got excessive material, parts or packaging? Have they cut down the amount of material used as much as possible?
Recycle	Have they used materials suitable for recycling? Is the product biodegradable or compostable? Has the product been made from recycled materials?
Reuse	Have they designed the product to be reused over and over? Have they built in a way that allows parts of the product to be used for another function?
Refuse	Are there any parts of the design that are completely unnecessary? Are there parts that have been added but would not affect the function?
Rethink	Have they considered all possible ways of achieving the outcome with this product? Is there a better, more environmentally friendly way to go about things?
Repair	Can parts of the product be replaced? Are those replacement parts commercially available? At end of use can it be separated into different material parts for ease of recycling?

Size

The designer of a product will have made important informed decisions about how large the product has been made. You can think of this in terms of length, width, depth and diameter. It's worth considering if it is unusually small or large for an object of its type.

To extend your answer, you could consider the size of the product's components. Parts such as grips, buttons and screens will have been sized with the user in mind. You might consider why the size choices have been made and if they are the most suitable choices.

Figure 3.6: Scale models of the Eiffel tower

Safety

For safety, you are considering how the designer has made sure the product is not dangerous to use. You might consider material choices, edges, weight and moving parts.

To extend your answer, you might consider health and safety guidance or legislation that would need to have been adhered to for that product type. You can consider what safety tests would have been required for the product to make it to sale. You should consider who uses the product too and where they use it. Products used by children have additional legislation and rules for safety, for example.

Figure 3.7: A glass bauble decoration with sharp shards

Function

For function, you need to identify what job the product has to do in order to be successful. You should try to ensure all analysed products have the same function to make the analysis useful and fair. The product may have more than one intended function and it's up to you to decide if this is important as part of your analysis.

To extend your answer you will compare it to similar products. You might consider what features on the product make it more effective at completing its role. You could look for similarities or differences in how the products achieve this function.

Materials

For materials, you should attempt to identify the materials used for the components of the product. In some situations, you may only be able to identify a general type, e.g. metal or polymer. If you look for recycling symbols or care instructions, you may be able to confirm specific material types.

To extend this answer you could consider the properties and care requirements associated with that material. You could consider why the designer chose that material over others. This might be a decision based on properties, appearance or cost. You might also be able to identify if the product was made from stock material shapes, e.g. sheets, rods or bars of materials, or was moulded or cast to achieve the design.

This leads onto manufacturing considerations. You should think about how the components were shaped and made. Usually the processes used have been chosen with the quality of finish and cost in mind.

Hands on!   1

You are now ready to analyse a product using ACCESS FM.

1   Find a product around you that you are quite familiar with. It might be something that you are wearing like a watch or shoes.

2   Write out ACCESS FM and what each letter stands for. Leave space to write next to each heading.

3   Analyse your chosen product using each category of ACCESS FM. Use the hints from the text to extend your description for each category.

Compare products

Analysing the information you have gathered using ACCESS FM will give you lots of positives and negatives for each of the products. You can write a short report on how these products compare to each other. To create some quantitative, measurable data to compare the products you can create some ranking tables.

Ranking matrices

Simple decision matrix

A simple decision matrix is a type of ranking matrix. Making a simple decision matrix just involves giving each product a score for each point of comparison. You have already used ACCESS FM, so it makes sense to use these headings (though you can add others). You can score them out of any number but you must score each product out of the same number. Keeping the maximum score the same allows you to quickly look for trends and themes.

Table 3.2: A simple decision matrix

	Product 1 Score (out of 10)	Product 2 Score	Product 3 Score
Aesthetics	5	7	9
Cost	9	8	9
Customer	4	7	8
Environment	5	7	7
Size	5	7	9
Safety	8	8	4
Function	6	6	8
Material	7	7	7
Total	49	57	61

Once you have scored all your products you can total the scores to give each product an overall score. The overall score gives a general idea of which product scored highly but doesn't necessarily give the best product.

In the example shown in Table 3.2 the products have been scored out of 10. Overall, Product 3 scores highest but has a very poor safety score that a client or customer might consider unacceptable.

To extend your answer you should look for situations where the scores are the same or unusually low or high and explain how this affects the overall impression of the product.

Weighted decision matrix

A weighted decision matrix works in a very similar way, scoring each product against each category. In a weighted decision matrix you can make some categories more important than others. When you calculate the total score for each category you multiply the score you gave by the weighting. This increases the total by a factor. In Table 3.3, aesthetics has been given a weighting of 1, which means it is not very important to us. In this example, the cost has been given a weighting of 2, meaning we think it is twice as important as the aesthetic appeal of this product. When calculating the score for the cost, we grade it as before but then multiply it by the weighting.

Table 3.3: Calculating a weighted decision matrix

	Weighting	×	Score	=	Total
			Product 1		
Aesthetics	1	×	5	=	5
Cost	2	×	9	=	18
Customer	2	×	4	=	8

In Table 3.4, Product 3 has the highest score even though it is unsafe. The weighted matrix can solve this if we put a higher weighting on safety. This alters both the safety scores and identifies Product 2 instead as the highest scoring.

Table 3.4: A weighted decision matrix

	Weighting	Product 1		Product 2		Product 3	
		Score	Total	Score	Total	Score	Total
Aesthetics	1	5	5	7	7	9	9
Cost	2	9	18	8	16	9	18
Customer	2	4	8	7	14	8	16
Environment	2	5	10	7	14	7	14
Size	2	5	10	7	14	9	18
Safety	5	8	40	8	40	4	20
Function	3	6	18	6	18	8	24
Material	2	7	14	7	14	7	14
Total			123		137		133

Be aware there is no rule or regulation dictating what the weightings should be. You have to make a decision based on which categories you feel are most important. It might also change between different product types. A machine in a factory, for example, might need a very high weighting on function and safety while a gift item might have a high weighting on aesthetics and customer.

Table 3.5: Advantages and disadvantages of ranking matrices

Advantages	Disadvantages
• Criteria can be set in advance using information from the client, desing brief and specification. • Allows for consistency when evaluating information from a range of testers. • Gives the designer a rating for the different design features, so can help them with development.	• Can become complex if produced for a detailed design. • Only gives numerical feedback, not ideas for development.

Table 3.6: Quality function deployment (QFD) matrix

Correlation matrix

+ +	Strong positive
+	Positive
_	Negative
_ _	Strong negative
	Not correlated

Relationship matrix

Symbol	Meaning	Value
⊙	Strong	9
○	Medium	3
△	Weak	1
	No assignment	0

	Customer importance rating (1 = low, 5 = high)	Percentage of customer importance rating	Design requirement 1	Design requirement 2	Design requirement 3	Design requirement 4	Design requirement 5	Design requirement 6	Design requirement 7	Design requirement 8	Comp 1	Comp 2	Comp 3	Comp 4
Customer need 1	1	4%		⊙	△		△	△		○	3	2	1	5
Customer need 2	2	13%	○	⊙						⊙	2	2	1	4
Customer need 3	3	16%				⊙	△				5	2	3	2
Customer need 4	3	13%		⊙	⊙	○		○	⊙	○	2	3	5	1
Customer need 5	4	16%	△	⊙	⊙	○	△	△	○	○	2	5	4	3
Customer need 6	3	12%	△	△	△	○				⊙	1	1	3	1
Customer need 7	4	23%	△	○	⊙	⊙			⊙		2	5	3	3
Customer need 8	5	20%		⊙		○	⊙	○			5	3	2	4
Importance score			1.04	5.64	4.12	4.32	2.12	1.16	3	2.76				
Percent of importance			4%	23%	17%	18%	9%	5%	12%	11%				

Competitor research

Quality function deployment (QFD)

Comparing products by quality function deployment (QFD) uses a more advanced matrix. It specifically uses what the customer prefers and requires as a criteria.

Down the left side are the customer needs. These could be a colour, size or special feature. Such information may be obtained from the design brief or from market research.

Across the top are the design requirements. These are the features that are needed in the final design. If, for example, the product requires a power source then one of the design requirements might be 'rechargeable batteries'.

The main part of the table is called the Relationship matrix. It is where the researcher cross-references each customer need with a design requirement and rates it as Weak, Medium or Strong. This helps identify which features to concentrate on and include in the design to fulfil the customers' requirements.

The "roof" of the table is called the interaction matrix. It identifies where the design requirements link to or depend on each other in some way. If there is a strong correlation, then it is marked with one or two plus (+) symbols. A blank space indicates that there is no link between them. Negative (–) symbols indicate that two requirements will prevent each other being met – for example, something being "heavy" means it is unlikely to also be "portable".

On the right of the table, competitor products are included as a point of reference. Each of these products is graded against the customer needs using a score (for example, 1–5). Keeping competitor products in mind when designing ensures your product will be competitive.

Table 3.7: Advantages and disadvantages of QFD

Advantages	Disadvantages
• Increases customer satisfaction by prioritising their requirements. • Improves the quality of products. • Allows for evaluation against measurable targets.	• Does not take other design factors into account, such as cost or time to produce a product. • Creating a QFD matrix can be complex and time-consuming.

Hands on!   2

You are now ready to use a matrix to analyse and compare products.

1   Collect several different pens from around you. If you are working with other people you could compare each other's. It helps if the pens are significantly different in some way.

2   Draw a ranking matrix using ACCESS FM like the example in Table 3.4. Assign each category a value for importance (5 = very important, 1 = not important).

3   Score each pen on each category of ACCESS FM and complete the weighted decision matrix. Where did each pen score highest? Which was the highest scoring product overall?

Stretch

Engineers must often analyse existing products to inform their own designing.

Find three different pens, use each one and take each one apart. Using comparison charts and ACCESS FM, produce a report explaining which of the pens is the most successful, and summarise the positive and negative features of the products.

1.2 Carry out product disassembly

Disassembling a product will do more than tell you what is inside it. You will be able to better analyse the material choices made, especially on components you couldn't previously see. It will give you clues about the processes used to make it and the assembly method used to put it together.

Safety is very important when disassembling products so ensure you consider the safety implications of taking apart the product and also the correct and safe use of any tools needed to complete the task.

There's only so much you can tell from the outside of a product. Engineers will often take apart competitors' products to discover more about them. This is called disassembly.

Use of manufacturer manuals or other published sources

You can usually find a surprising amount of information about products in the manual provided with them. Usually you can find:

- company information

- instructions for use

- material choice

- maintenance requirements

- safety issues

- disposal information

- other associated products

- spare parts available.

Figure 3.8: Private aircraft engineer using manuals before undertaking repairs

More complex products will also have additional documents available. Large engineered products such as cars have additional maintenance manuals produced by third parties. The internet will also have guides, blogs and videos regarding the repair, taking apart or maintenance of almost all common products.

All safety issues raised in these documents need to be identified and noted before any physical disassembly takes place.

Over to you!

1   Do an internet search for your model of mobile phone. Add the terms 'teardown' or 'disassembly' to the search. Are there videos or sites detailing the disassembly of your device? Try listing the types of information they show/tell you.

2   Search the company website for your phone. List the relevant documents that are available. Can you find a replacement manual for your phone? See what information it contains about maintenance and repair.

3   Search shopping sites for your phone. What parts are available for it? Often mobile phones require specific tools to change and disassemble parts. See if you can source the tools required to complete a replacement of these parts.

Use appropriate tools and instruments

Many engineered products use temporary fixings (screws, clips and bolts) that can be taken apart to enable maintenance or recycling. This helps when disassembling a product. Before disassembly, you need to research and gather the correct tools. There are many different types of screws and bolts, with many different types of heads and in many different sizes.

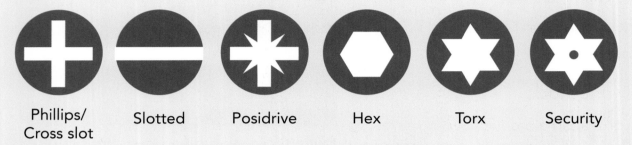

Phillips/Cross slot   Slotted   Posidrive   Hex   Torx   Security

Figure 3.9: Some common screw head types

You should record which tools you are going to use to disassemble the product. You should also research any safety guidelines and protective equipment required.

If parts of the product have been permanently fastened, e.g. with glue or welded, you will have to make an informed decision on whether you continue to open up the product with a suitable method or not.

Analyse the disassembled product

Components and their functions

Once you have taken the product apart, you can look at what each part does. In the case of electronics and circuits it isn't necessary to have an in-depth idea of how the circuit is actually programmed, just its general function.

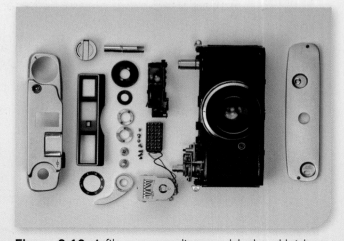

Figure 3.10: A film camera disassembled and laid out

For each part you analyse the function of, you should consider the following:

- What the component does and how it contributes to the overall product.

- If the quality of the component is of similar quality to or better than the other parts. Parts that move or are load or stress bearing are more likely to wear or fail.

- If the component has been made to a larger tolerance than the parts around it.

Assembly methods

When you take apart a product it will give you clues as to how it was assembled. You will discover whether temporary fixings such as screws or clips were used or if more permanent methods such as gluing or soldering were used. To record this, keep a record or diary of tools you use to take each piece apart.

Many products are designed for manufacture and assembly (DFMA). This means the assembly method has been designed to be relatively fast and use fewer parts. To extend your answer you could explain how the assembly method has made the product quicker to make, or suitable for repair.

Materials

As you take the product apart you will be able to look at the materials used more clearly. Different materials have different properties so the product will not be made from just one material. Metals are often used for strength and ductility when making fixings like screws, for example. Polymers are often used where complex shapes are required as they are easily shaped.

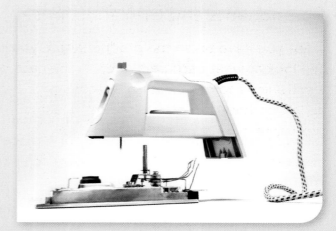

Figure 3.11: An exploded view of a typical electric iron

To extend your answer, explain why the chosen materials have properties suitable for the component. You could research possible alternative materials to identify if they are the best choice.

Production methods

By identifying the shape of the components and the materials, you can start to work out the method used to make each part. This will require a bit of research and practice too. There is often more than one way to make each part so you could extend your answer by explaining if this is the most suitable method to make it.

Maintenance considerations

Most products need some level of maintenance. In our everyday lives we probably do this without thinking about it: cleaning football boots after use, for example, or lubricating skateboard trucks. In electronic products, batteries can usually be accessed so they can be changed. In industrial situations, like factories or maintaining large vehicles, these routines are more important and usually scheduled and documented. Nobody wants a cruise ship's engine to seize up in the middle of the ocean or a theme park ride to start rattling.

Engineers design their products with the ability to maintain them in mind. Temporary fixings, access hatches or compartments are often built in to allow a user to check, clean, repair or replace parts. When doing your disassembly you should identify how each part has been designed for maintenance by the designer.

You could ask yourself the following questions.

• How accessible is a component? Can it be reached to undertake maintenance tasks? This is most important for parts that will need cleaning, checking or replacing. Filters on vacuum cleaners are usually easy to access, for example, as they quickly collect dirt and dust that needs removing.

- Can a component be replaced? Has the part been designed to be switched out for a new one? Are the replacement parts readily available? This is particularly important for parts that move or will experience wear. On a bike, for example, almost all parts are replaceable.

- Does a part need to be cleaned? Will a component build up dirt, grease or grime and if so can it be cleaned in situ or can it be removed for cleaning?

Case study

The development of the Land Rover

The Land Rover is an iconic design. It was originally shown at an automobile show in Amsterdam on April 30, 1948. Its designer, Maurice Wilks, used an ex-army American Jeep on his farm. He thought it was an excellent agricultural vehicle, because it was 4×4, and also versatile like a car.

Figure 3.12 and Figure 3.13: A Jeep and a Land Rover. What similarities and differences can you see between them?

The Jeep was designed for battlefield situations so was designed to be very rugged. It was also designed for disassembly. It was recognised that the Jeep might need to be repaired in remote locations and without access to the correct parts, so it was easy to strip down and parts were easy to replicate, exchange or produce wherever possible.

Continued

Through his own experience and reverse engineering, Maurice Wilks took the good features of the Jeep and eliminated many of the mechanical problems it had, creating the Series 1 Land Rover. It was so stripped down that initially seat cushions and doors were optional extras.

The design was incredibly popular and was used by police, military, aid workers and off-road explorers. By 1976, Rover had produced one million of the vehicles.

Check your understanding

1   What were the advantages to having and using a Jeep before designing the Land Rover?

2   What were the desirable features Wilks wanted to reproduce in his own vehicle?

3   What would Wilks have been able to identify by disassembly of the Jeep on his farm that he could not have discovered otherwise?

Review your learning

Test your knowledge   3

1   What does disassembly mean?

2   Explain what ACCESS FM is.

3   Justify how an engineering matrix helps to identify the strengths and weaknesses of products.

What have you learnt?

	See section
• How to use ACCESS FM to analyse key features of a product.	1.1
• How to describe the strengths and weaknesses of existing products.	1.2
• How to use an engineering matrix effectively.	1.2

TA2

Modelling design ideas

Let's get started

Do you remember making junk models like rockets or robots out of cereal boxes and kitchen rolls? The model was much smaller than the real thing would be. Parts of the model would work, parts would not, some materials would be substituted, e.g. card instead of sheet metal.

These rules set the stage for designers engineering new products, too. They are hoping to convey an idea. They might make models to scale, or use card, foam or computer modelling. They might make models that don't function just to show what a product might look like.

What will you learn?

- How to produce a comprehensive CAD design.

- How to plan a practical making process, including planning for safety.

- How to undertake a practical making process, working independently and safely.

- How to review your product and evaluate how it meets the specification.

- How to review your own making and identify any areas you could improve upon.

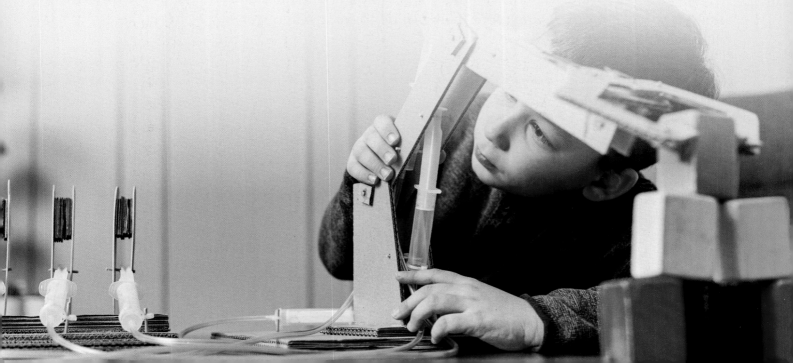

2.1 Methods of modelling

For the second part of the non-exam assessment (NEA), you will design and model a product based on a provided design specification. Your product will be similar in function to the ones you analysed so far and should be based on your findings. Hopefully you will have identified enough positive features and possible improvements to give you some inspiration. If you haven't, it might be worth reviewing your analysis and disassembly work to create a list of desirable qualities.

Through modelling, you are going to create a computer-generated model and then plan and make a prototype of the design. Because you are going to make it, it is very helpful if you have in mind possible materials and manufacturing methods right from the start. That way you won't design something that will be impractical to make later on.

To extend your answers, it would also be worth considering designs suitable for production on a suitable scale of manufacture. If you were designing a bike light, for example, they are often batch or mass produced, so you may wish to consider designs that could use materials and processes that could take place in these quantities.

Virtual CAD 3D

You need to produce a CAD model of your product idea for the NEA. Because you are going to be making this model, you need to think about the shapes and parts you are designing and keep manufacturing methods and possible materials in mind. The more parts, details and images you can produce, the more there will be to work with once you start making.

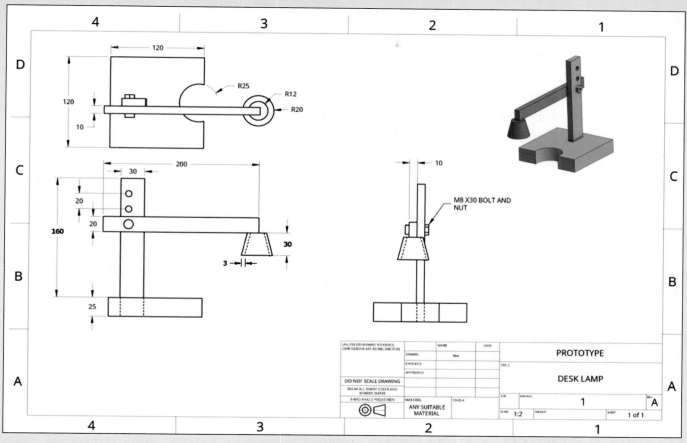

Figure 3.14: CAD drawing of a product design

Create a 3D model using CAD 3D software

Single components

Most products are made up of components made in different ways and from different materials. Because of this, single component 3D models are useful. You can refer to these diagrams and models as you make each part.

Assemblies of items to form a product

CAD assemblies are when you place all of the components of the design together in the arrangement they are supposed to go in, creating a 3D model of your completed design. This is useful to ensure pieces fit together in the dimensions you have designed them in. This can prevent errors in scale or part design before you start making.

Animation and simulation

Animations and simulations are used to give more information about a design. Engineers can animate 3D CAD models to prototype how the design might move, extend or alter when in operation. Simulations can demonstrate the assembly process, the operation of the product or simulate working conditions.

Some 3D software allows you to animate the individual components so they move independently. This can be used to create an assembly animation. You could demonstrate how each component slots together and is fastened to create the final assembly. This kind of animation would be useful in planning the assembly of the design.

Most 3D software will allow you to move points of the design. This can be used to produce an animation of how the product operates. For example, you could animate a robot arm in motion or show how gears turn in a mechanism. This kind of simulation would be useful in describing the operation of the product and would help check it will function correctly.

Figure 3.15: A robot arm could be animated in CAD to show how it moves

Simulations can be used to simulate a wide range of effects, including tension and torsion forces, wear and tear, heat transfer and aerodynamics. They can also be used to simulate how an object interacts with other objects.

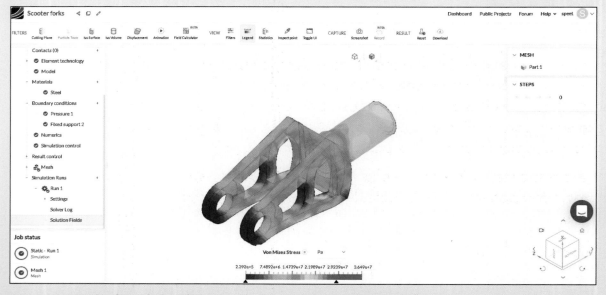

Figure 3.16: The front forks of a scooter with compressive force simulated

Figure 3.16 shows a compressive force being simulated on part of the model as if it is in use. The red and orange areas identify the parts under most stress and therefore the areas most likely to fail. Engineers can use this information to improve the design, address safety concerns or identify the best use for the product.

Test your knowledge   1

1   Identify the purpose of producing a 3D CAD model.

2   Explain what multiple part assemblies are.

3   Justify why a design with moving parts might need a simulation.

Over to you!   1

Unscrew your pen and lay the parts out in front of you.

1   Create a 3D model of the pen by modelling each part and putting them together.

2   Get someone else to look at the model. Does it make sense to them? Are there any inaccuracies they can see?

3   List all the parts it is made from, and the materials used for each part.

Physical modelling

Select an appropriate modelling method

Before starting your physical models, you should consider the method you might use. It is likely your components will require a range of manufacturing methods – as in industry it won't be appropriate for one process to make every part. Having a range of modelling methods is good because it allows you to demonstrate your planning and making skills.

You may also have some standard components in your design: screws, bolts and electronic components, for example. It's fine not to attempt to manufacture these.

Sheet and block modelling

You may use sheet and **block modelling** to make a representation of your design. Sheet modelling is using materials that traditionally come in flat stock forms to make a model. Block modelling is using solid blocks of material to carve a model out of.

The model might be made using the actual materials you have chosen to use. You can model using polymers and metals, for example. These materials require special tools and machines to shape and form them.

Sometimes you will not be able to use the actual materials. Some materials are expensive, take too much time to work or require specialist machinery or processes that are just not available to you. In these situations, you might use modelling materials such as card, paper and foam. These types of model can still show:

- how a product might look
- the form of the product and how it fits together
- the size and scale of the product.

To make these models, you must use the tools, machines and processes available to you. You might want to use injection moulding, for example. However, if you don't have access to the process, it is fine to use an alternative method and explain how the model would be manufactured in industry.

Breadboarding

If your product has an electronic aspect to it then breadboarding is an excellent way of modelling this is. A breadboard can demonstrate you to show how electronic circuits might work in the final manufactured product. For more complex processes, programmable chips can be used in place of the PCBs that might exist in the final design.

Figure 3.17: A circuit built on a breadboard

Your breadboard will not, of course, look like the final design. It is intended to show the function of a part of the product. Typically, you would produce this type of model alongside a physical model.

3D printing

3D printing is an excellent way of producing complex or unusual shapes. This process is usually too slow for most industrial uses, especially on a large scale, but is commonly used in the creation of initial models or prototypes by engineers and designers.

It is a good substitute for parts that would be injection moulded or made using CNC machinery you might not have access to. It allows you to demonstrate the part in a similar material and explain how it might be created using a different method on a production line.

Test your knowledge   2

1   Give two purposes of physical modelling.

2   Explain when using breadboarding would be an appropriate modelling method.

3   Describe an advantage and a disadvantage of 3D printing to produce a model.

Over to you!   2

1   Use paper and card to model a simple mobile phone stand. Don't sketch it first – just use sheet modelling to develop your ideas.

2   Use block foam to model a handle of a games controller. Practise curved and rounded shapes that fit your hand.

3   Compare the two modelling methods. Why would the stand have been harder to model in foam? Why would the games controller have been harder to model from sheet material?

Select and use appropriate materials, processes, tools and equipment to produce a prototype

Before making your models, you should decide upon the steps you are going to take. Engineering designers will often produce a very detailed manufacturing plan. Often, they need to explain to another engineer or a team how to make it as they will not be the one making it.

For each component you are making you should detail how you are going to make the model for it. Your manufacturing plan could be a detailed table, a series of paragraphs, a flowchart or a combination of all three. It should include details about materials, process, quality control and time.

Materials

You should clearly identify what material each component will be made out of. You should explain why you believe it to be a suitable choice for this component.

To extend your answer, you can explain what stock form the material comes in that you are going to use. Metals, for example, come in a wide selection of sheets, plates, bars and rods. You should detail the stock form you are going to use for the current process.

Figure 3.18: Raw materials in a range of stock forms

Process

Each process will be a separate stage of your planning. It should detail an activity you will undertake in the production of the components of your product. Some examples of activities you might include are:

- **Preparing for an activity** For example, setting up and preheating machinery such as a vacuum former or hot wire cutter. To extend your answer, include details such as specific temperatures or settings.

- **Undertaking a shaping process** Using a specific hand tool or machine to cut or form a piece of material. To extend your answer, you could detail how to specifically use the equipment in this situation and why this specific process and equipment have been chosen.

- **Undertaking a finishing process** This might include polishing, sanding or painting, for example. It could involve a chemical treatment. To extend your answer, you could explain how to apply the finish and the anticipated effect you hope to achieve.

- **Undertake an assembly process** This might include using temporary fixings such as screws or bolts. It might involve a permanent fixing method such as using a glue or solvent.

There are many other possible activities you could identify that are specific to your own design. You should detail the processes needed as if someone else was going to make it for you.

Quality control

When should you stop sanding a piece of work? How tight is too tight when tightening a bolt? You should identify what checks you can make at each stage to ensure fewer things go wrong work and improve the chance of the final product being successful.

Figure 3.19: Quality control taking place in a factory

- **Quality control** A check you complete while you are making, such as ensuring a component is in tolerance, making sure a finish is smooth or checking a temperature is correct. To extend your answer, explain what action you might take if the outcome doesn't pass the quality control check. This might involve repeating a process or starting a whole component again.

- **Quality assurance** A check you make once a part or product has been completed. You should detail these checks as each component is completed and once the whole product is complete.

Time

In engineering, a manufacturing plan is often accompanied by a time plan. This sets out the expected duration of each task and so also gives an idea how long the whole product will take to make. This allows the manufacturing to stay on track.

It is impossible to accurately predict the length of each activity before you do it so you should just make the best estimate for each step and if necessary give yourself more time than you think you will need.

Figure 3.20: A manufacturing time plan

Apply safe working procedures when making the prototype

In any manufacturing, either in a workshop or in industry, there is an element of risk. It's important that this risk is investigated and any way of reducing the risk is put in place.

Identifying risk

Risks can be graded by their severity and their likelihood.

- **Likelihood** The chance of an injury happening. Likely means it is quite possible an injury might occur. An example of a likely injury is jabbing yourself with a needle when sewing or burning yourself when soldering.

- **Severity** Risks that are considered severe have serious consequences. They may cause serious injury. Examples of a serious injury might be a chemical that causes damage when inhaled or burns caused by casting or welding.

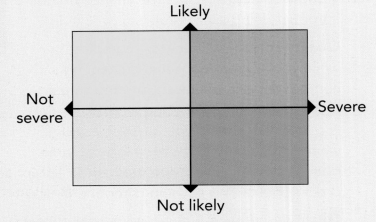

Figure 3.21: Severity versus likelihood

Risks that are not severe and not likely do not require special consideration. They are probably not going to happen and if they do will have few consequences.

You should preare for risks that are likely but not severe. Although the consequences are not serious, you know there is a good chance of them happening so you must make sure you take any steps needed to limit the chances of them happening.

Risks that are severe but not likely also need preparations putting in place. You know that they probably won't happen but if they do there could be serious injury. You must take any steps to limit the chance of them happening and have the necessary equipment ready in case they do.

Risks that are both severe and likely should be avoided. Unless you can take precautions to reduce the risk, these activities can't be done as they are likely to result in significant harm.

In industry a risk matrix, like Table 3.8, is often used to identify risk as part of a **risk assessment**.

Table 3.8: A risk matrix

Risk matrix		Consequence				
		1 Insignificant	2 Minor	3 Moderate	4 Major	5 Catastrophic
Likelihood	5 Almost certain	High	High	Extreme	Extreme	Extreme
	4 Likely	Moderate	High	High	Extreme	Extreme
	3 Moderate	Low	Moderate	High	Extreme	Extreme
	2 Unlikely	Low	Low	Moderate	High	Extreme
	1 Rare	Low	Low	Moderate	High	High

Controlling risk

Controlling risk is about preparing to undertake a process in the safest way possible. Where a risk can't be avoided altogether, it can be minimised by planning ahead.

- **Preparation** These safety considerations involve setting up the area you are going to work in. You might consider ventilation, lighting and space depending on the task that is going to take place. These safety considerations also involve setting up the workspace for the specific process. You might ensure that the area is tidy or free of flammable objects for heat processes. You might need to ensure safety equipment such as water, fire extinguishers or eyebaths is available.

- **Working** These safety considerations involve working safely. You may need certain personal protective equipment (PPE) such as gloves, goggles or a dust mask. There will certainly be safe practices depending on the tools or equipment being used.

- **Afterwards** These safety considerations are about securing the working area safely again. Clearing up any waste and spills, and securing chemicals could be examples of this.

To help you write risk assessments for the processes you have planned, you can consult professional health and safety documentation from other organisations. You could also consult controlled substance data sheets. The hierarchy of controls shown in Figure 3.23 is also used in industry and useful when assessing risk. When writing your risk assessments, you start at the top of the pyramid and work down. The higher up the pyramid, the more effective the safety consideration. For example, using a less risky alternative process (tier 2) is safer than doing an unsafe practice with PPE (tier 5).

Figure 3.22: A clean, spacious, well-lit, well-ventilated and organised workshop will provide a safe working environment

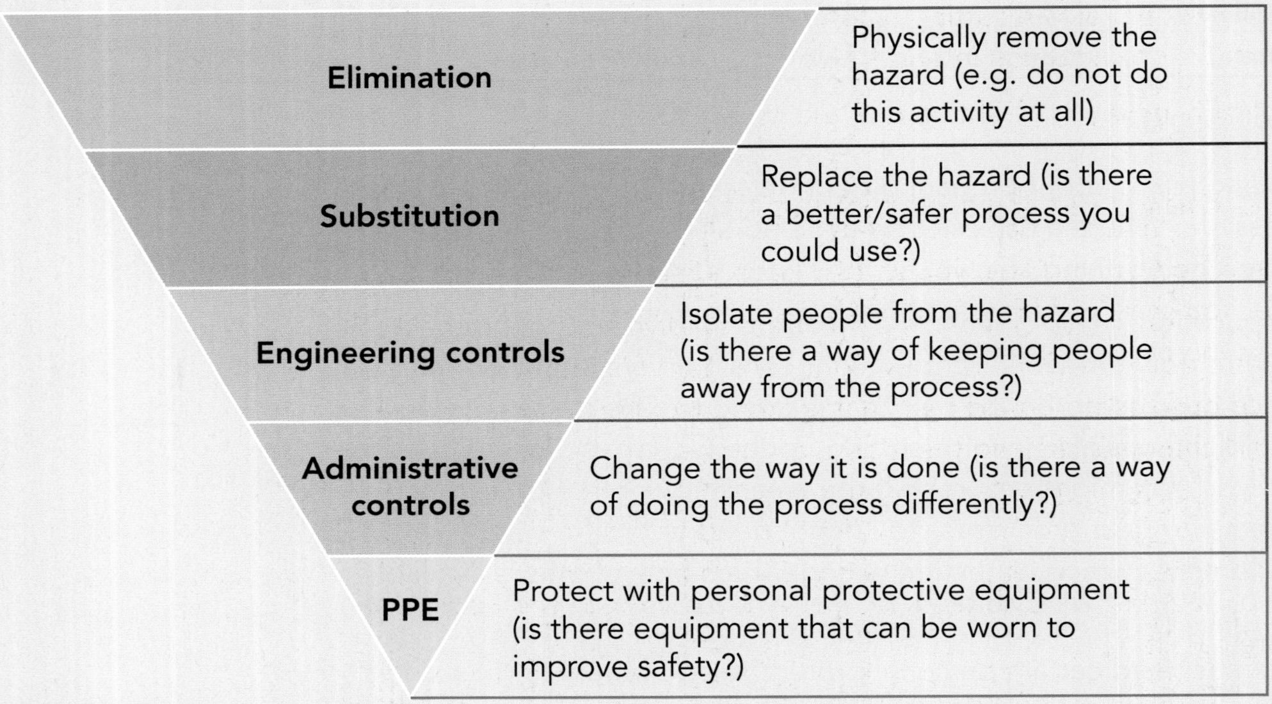

Elimination	Physically remove the hazard (e.g. do not do this activity at all)
Substitution	Replace the hazard (is there a better/safer process you could use?)
Engineering controls	Isolate people from the hazard (is there a way of keeping people away from the process?)
Administrative controls	Change the way it is done (is there a way of doing the process differently?)
PPE	Protect with personal protective equipment (is there equipment that can be worn to improve safety?)

Figure 3.23: Hierarchy of control

For any practical activity, you should record both the risks you have perceived and the measures you have put in place to control the risks. You might do this as a chart, a guide or a piece of extended writing.

Test your knowledge   3

1 State two ways you can grade a risk.

2 Describe why it is important to seek ways to minimise risk.

3 Explain how you can control risk using a hierarchy of control.

Over to you!   3

Consider cutting a simple shape out of MDF (medium density fibreboard) using hand tools.

1 Identify the risks that may be present in this task and attempt to grade how likely and severe those risks might be.

2 Plan setting up the cutting task, considering how you would prepare the area you intend to work in.

3 Identify how you might control the risks involved.

Record the key stages of making the prototype

While making your models, you should keep a record of the processes you use. You should refer to your manufacturing plan and risk assessments regularly. In your notes mention:

*   which processes worked particularly well and which processes you would change if making the model again

*   which processes you would change for the actual manufacture of the product

*   if the materials were suitable or if an alternative material would be more suitable

*   any difficulties experienced due to your own experience with the tools or machinery.

Taking photos or short videos of your practice is also necessary during these stages. At this point, you should also record any changes that had to happen to make the manufacturing possible.

Compare the prototype against the product design specification

This is the first part of an evaluation task. You will need to finish all your planning and making before you can undertake it.

You should compare your models/prototypes with the specification. For each point you should:

- describe factually what your design has done
- describe how it meets the specification point
- explain what evidence there is that it meets the specification point
- identify what could be done to better meet the specification point.

By following these points, you should create a few sentences and some justified points for each of the specification points. You can either do this through continuous writing or using a table.

Identify potential improvements in the design

For the second part of your evaluation, you should identify potential improvements in the design.

Design improvements For any area of the specification your design did not fully meet, you should explain how the design might be modified to better meet that point.

Planning and manufacturing improvements Some issues with the final outcome may be due to issues in the making. You should identify any areas where your manufacturing skills could be improved to improve the outcome. This might include further training or practise on an existing machine, or training on a more suitable piece of machinery.

Suitability for manufacturing You should also identify how the design might be modified to be suitable for production. This might include reducing the number of parts, reducing the number of making stages, changing the number of pre-manufactured components or choosing an alternative manufacturing method. This is especially important if your production method used a lot of foam, card, 3D printing or other methods or materials that would not be suitable for production.

Case study

The Millennium Dome

The Millennium Dome (also known as The O2 Arena) was an engineering project designed to mark the year 2000, built in Greenwich, London. It is a massive covered structure – the eighth largest building in the world by useable volume.

The unique design of the dome required extensive modelling and prototyping to test the idea before it was produced. No open structure of this scale and design had ever been produced before and the scale and cost of the project made it impossible to test the idea full size.

Modelling had to prove the design would not fail. The lightweight structure of the roof weighs less than the air it contains but is also freely supported by cables from twelve towers.

The purpose, size and design of the dome also changed during its design. Plans included an exhibition space, a hotel, a hospital, shops and apartments. Models were used to plan these different design iterations. Presentations of these ideas had to be produced for approval.

Figure 3.24: The Millennium Dome in Greenwich

Figure 3.25: The O2 Arena being constructed

CAD simulations of the dome were produced.

After a rigorous process of modelling, the final product was manufactured in 15 months based on the models and was manufactured under budget.

Check your understanding

1   Identify what types of modelling allowed the Millennium Dome project to be realised.

2   Explain why modelling is important before constructing a project of this scale.

3   Justify who the models would have been presented to along the process of developing the final idea.

Stretch

Modelling a design helps engineers visualise and test their ideas.

Using card, model a controller for an existing games console that is intended to be used one handed. You can start by holding an existing games controller in one hand and then think about how it would need to be gripped and where the buttons should be placed to allow the same functionality with just one hand.

Choose a material to make one of your designs full size and try holding it. Write a short report on how it is suitable and how it might be further improved.

Review your learning

Test your knowledge   4

1   Identify why producing a 3D CAD model first helps when making a physical model.

2   Explain why engineers analyse existing products before designing their own.

3   Explain what information might be included in a manufacturing plan.

4   Justify the need to evaluate a model once it has been produced.

What have you learnt?

	See section
• How to produce a detailed CAD design.	2.1
• How to plan a practical making process, taking safety into account.	2.1
• How to work safely and independently while undertaking a practical making process.	2.1
• How to review and evaluate your product against the specification.	2.1
• How to review your own making and identify areas for improvement.	2.1

Glossary

2D: Two-dimensional (flat) components with features defined using X and Y coordinates.

3D: Three-dimensional components with features defined using X, Y and Z coordinates.

Abbreviation: A shortened form of a word or phrase. In engineering design, it is often a letter or symbol used to represent a design feature.

ACCESS FM: Mnemonic for remembering and describing the key points covered by the design specification. Stands for: Aesthetics, Cost, Customer, Environment, Size, Safety, Function and Materials.

Aesthetics: The way a product reacts with the senses, defining pleasing qualities.

Alloy: A mixture of two metals or elements.

Animation: Method to create the illusion of movement.

Annotation: Comments added to a sketch to explain the sketch to a reader.

Anthropometrics: The study of measurements of the human body.

Anthropometrist: A scientist who deals with anthropometry: the measurement of the size, weight and proportions of the human body.

Assembly: A process of fitting components together to make a whole product.

Assembly drawing: Drawing showing how separate components fit together.

Batch production: Manufacturing of products in specific amounts (a batch).

Block diagram: Diagram of products or systems where separate parts are represented by blocks connected by lines showing their relationship to one another.

Block modelling: Using blocks of material to create a 3D representation of a design or part of a design.

Breadboard: Used to build and test circuits quickly before finalising any circuit design.

Breadboarding: A way of testing electronic circuits on a solderless construction base called a breadboard.

British Standards: Standards that products must conform to, produced by the BSI (British Standards Institution).

Cabinet oblique: A method of representing a 3D object on paper by extending the depth of the drawing using lines at 45 degrees. The receding axis (the depth) is drawn at half size to appear visually similar to the object.

Capital costs: Starting costs of setting up a facility to manufacture a product.

Card modelling: Used to create real-life models; needs minimal equipment and only basic resources.

Cavalier oblique: A method of representing a 3D object on paper by extending the depth of the drawing using lines at 45 degrees. The receding axis (the depth) is drawn at full size.

Circuit diagram: Graphical representation of an electric circuit, showing how separate electrical components are connected.

Circular economy: A system that reduces the impact of materials on the environment by reducing waste and pollution and maximising the reuse of materials.

Computer aided design (CAD): Software that allows 2D drawings and 3D models to be produced on screen with different parts and modelled in different materials.

Design brief: A short summary of the design context and the main user requirements.

Design specification: A detailed list that gives clear and specific requirements for the product being designed so it can match the design brief. See also: ACCESS FM.

Design strategy: A method for designing a product.

Diameter: Distance across a circle.

Dimensions: Numerical values used in engineering drawings to specify the sizes or positions of key features (measurements are usually in millimetres).

Disassembly: Taking something apart, for example, a piece of equipment or product; often to repair, replace or recycle components.

Ergonomic design: The design of anything that involves people.

Ergonomics: Arranging or designing a product in a way that enables people to interact with it more efficiently or safely, often using anthropometric data as a reference.

Evaluation: Checking a design or product to ensure it will work as intended and matches the design brief and specification.

Exploded view: Drawing where the components of a product are drawn slightly separated from each other and suspended in space to show their relationship or the order of assembly.

Extrude tool: CAD tool used to create a 3D solid object by pulling a 2D profile sketch along an axis.

Ferrous metals: Metals or alloys which contain iron.

Finishing: A process that changes the surface of a material in a useful way, either protective or decorative.

Flowchart: Block diagram that shows how various processes are linked together to achieve a specific outcome.

Forming: A process that changes the shape of a material without a change of state.

Freehand sketching: Drawing without the use of measuring instruments.

Functional anthropometry: The recording of measurements taken from body positions when moving or undertaking an activity. For example, the reach or angle of rotation when moving arms to complete a task or the dimensions of a person in a crawling stance.

Inclusive design: Designing products to be usable by as many different people as possible without special modifications.

International standards: Standards created by the ISO (International Organization for Standardization).

Isometric drawing: 3D pictorial drawing that focuses on the edge of an object and uses an angle of 30 degrees to the horizontal.

Iterative design: The development of a product through modelling and repeated testing.

Joining: A process that is used to attach separate pieces of material together.

Label: Used to identify separate components in a sketch.

Labour costs: Costs of paying people to make the product.

Legislation: Laws proposed by the government and made official by Acts of Parliament

Linear design: The development of a product through a series of sequential stages.

Linear measurements: Show the dimensions of a part or product in mm. Recorded with lines and arrows.

Longevity: The useful life of a product, from manufacture until its eventual disposal.

Machined finish: The surface roughness left on a material after shaping it with a cutting tool. Measured in μm.

Manufacturing processes: Processes that are used to make products. See also: Wasting, Shaping, Forming, Joining, Finishing and Assembly.

Market pull: When a need for a product arises from consumer demand which 'pulls' the development of a new product.

Mass production: Rapid production of standardised products and components, often on a production line.

Mechanical features: Common features of a product's or component's shape or form, such as holes, threads, chamfers, countersinks and knurls; displayed on drawings using standard markings so they are easy to identify.

Mechanical performance: Refers to how a component will move and fuction. CAD software can be used to show whether the product would function as intended in real life.

Model: A three dimensional object that demonstrates the look and feel of a design.

Modelling: Creating a three-dimensional object that demonstrates the look and feel of a design and allows the designer to check proportions, scale and function of the design.

Needs: Characteristics that a product must have.

Non-ferrous metals: Metals or alloys which do not contain iron.

Objective: Unbiased. For example, objective measurements are results that are taken impartially.

Oblique drawing: 3D pictorial drawing that focuses on the face of an object and uses an angle of 45 degrees to the horizontal.

One-off production: Manufacturing products one at a time.

Orthographic drawing: Projection drawing that shows an object from every angle to help manufacturers plan production. Uses several 2D projections (or views) to represent a 3D object. See also Orthographic projection.

Orthographic projection: See Orthographic drawing.

Overheads: General costs of running a business, not directly attributed to a particular product or service.

Physical modelling: Creating a real model using a range of materials including card, clay, wood or additive manufacturing.

Planned obsolescence: A policy of producing consumer goods that rapidly become obsolete, due to changes in design or stopping supply of spare parts.

Primary research: Research that deals directly with potential or existing customers. It can include surveys, focus groups and interviews.

Production costs: Overall cost of making a product.

Product requirements: Features the product should have or include, developed from research and described in the design specification.

Prosecuted: Officially accused in a court of breaking the law.

Prototype: A model of a product used to test the design idea to see if it functions as intended.

Qualitative: Data based on descriptions, observations or opinions.

Qualitative comparison: Information collected through observations, interviews and from examining and comparing the design idea with the design brief and specification.

Quality function deployment (QFD): A design tool that helps transform the customers' needs and wants into a product design and a method for evaluating ideas.

Quantitative: Data based on numerical facts.

Quantitative comparison: Comparing numerical data from a model against factual data within the design brief and specification.

Radius: The distance from the centre of a circle to its edge.

Ranking matrix: Used as a tool to help make decisions when comparing products or when evaluating a product or design idea; provides set criteria for evaluation (plural: Ranking matrices).

Rendering: A CAD tool used to add visual effects, e.g. material types to an object.

Reusability: Using an object again, for its original intended purpose or for an alternative use.

Revolve tool: A CAD tool used to create cylindrical shapes.

Risk assessment: Identifies risks and describes ways and procedures to stop accidents happening.

Scale: Amount by which a drawing is enlarged or reduced from the actual size of an object, shown as a ratio.

Scale of manufacture: The quantity of product/parts to be made which determines the manufacturing process.

Secondary research: Research that is based on data that has already been gathered and is often publicly available.

Shaping: A process that involves a change of state of the material.

Shell tool: A CAD tool used to hollow out the inside of a 3D solid object.

Simulation: Imitation of a real product by looks and function.

Sketch: Freehand drawing used as part of the design ideas for a product.

Standard: Agreed way of doing something such as making a product or providing a service.

Standard conventions: Agreed rules that set the standards used in engineering, e.g. drawing conventions in BS EN 8888.

Stock forms: The profiles a material is commonly available in, for example, sheets or tubes.

Structural anthropometry: The recording of physical measurements of the body. For example, the height of a body when standing or sitting, or the weight of a body.

Subjective: Based on personal opinion or preference.

Surface finish (machining): Engineered surface finish is the smoothness or roughness of the face of a material.

Sustainable design: The development of a product that uses environmentally friendly methods to not harm people or the planet.

Technology push: When new technology is created, it can lead to the development of new products that are 'pushed' onto the market.

Texture: The surface quality used to add realism to a sketch.

Third angle orthographic projection: A drawing showing three different views of a part in 2D (front, plan and side) on the same diagram.

Title block: Area on a drawing which contains important information about the drawing or part.

Tolerance: The variation allowed between a specified dimension in an engineering design and the measured dimension on the finished component.

Tone: The increase/decrease of light to dark from one part of a sketch to another.

User-centred design (UCD): The development of a product to meet the requirements of a specific user or small group of users.

Virtual modelling: A computer generated representation of a design created using CAD software. See also: Simulation.

Wants: Characteristics that are desirable in a product but not essential.

Wasting: A process that removes material.

Wiring diagram: Simplified pictorial representation of a circuit that shows how the components should be connected together.

Work plane: A 2D surface used as the origin for a view.

Index